Orphans
Charles D'Ambrosio

clear cut press

Astoria, Oregon

Designed by Tae Won Yu
Copyedited by Allison Dubinsky

Printed and Bound in Japan by Toppan Printing Co. Ltd.

ORPHANS / Charles D'Ambrosio

ISBN 0-9723234-5-7

Library of Congress Control Number: 2004111421

Clear Cut Press is grateful to its subscribers for their support.

Clear Cut Press
P.O. Box 623
Astoria, Oregon 97103
www.clearcutpress.com

Acknowledgments

"The Crime That Never Was," "Seattle, 1974," "Mary Kay Letourneau," and "Whaling" all appeared in the *Stranger* between 1994 and 1997. "Seattle, 1974" also appeared in *The Eleventh Draft: Craft and the Writing Life from the Iowa Writers' Workshop*, ed. Frank Conroy (HarperCollins, 1999). "Modular Homes," "Brick Wall," "Hell House," "Biosquat," and "Orphans" all appeared in *Nest* magazine between 1999 and 2004. "Brick Wall" was also published in *Harper's* in November 2001. "Documents" was published in the *New Yorker* in 2003. "Degrees of Gray" was written for the anthology *The Clear Cut Future* (Clear Cut Press, 2003).

"Communion," by Sherman Alexie, was published in *The Man Who Loves Salmon* (Limberlost Press, 1998).

"Degrees of Gray in Philipsburg," by Richard Hugo, appears with permission of Ripley Hugo. It was also published in *Making Certain It Goes On: Collected Poems of Richard Hugo* (W. W. Norton, 1984).

The quotations from the work of Czeslaw Milosz in "Degrees of Gray" are taken from Milosz's books *Native Realm: A Search for Self-definition* (University of California Press, 1981), *New and Collected Poems 1931-2001* (HarperCollins, 2001), and *To Begin Where I Am: Selected Essays* (FSG, 2002). His quotations from the work of Joseph Brodsky are taken from Brodsky's *Collected Poems in English* (FSG, 2000), *On Grief and Reason: Essays* (FSG, 1996), and *Less Than One: Selected Essays* (FSG, 1986). His quote from Erich Auerbach is from Auerbach's *Mimesis: The Representation of Reality in Western Literature* (Princeton University Press, 1953).

For Drew Bouton

Contents

Orphans

The Crime That Never Was

This is totally false, but for the sake of the story let's say the events in question begin around 2 AM, just because that's when I show up on the scene. The events as I find them are fairly meaty by big-league journalistic standards, involving domestic violence, assault and battery, a hostage, a gunman—all of which, I realize, could easily (and most often does) play itself out in lonely, tragic, and unobserved ways, but there's also, this night, cordons of yellow police ribbon closing off several blocks in Belltown, maybe fifty cops, a spooky anti-riot-terrorist vehicle the color of some nightmare rodent, plus a ruck of TV news reporters and their retinue of technicians. This guy—the Bad Guy— apparently thought he was just going to drink a few beers and bounce his girlfriend against the walls and go to sleep, but instead of a little quiet and intimate extracurricular abuse before bed he's now got major civic apparatus marshaling for a siege outside his window. No sleep for him tonight, and no more secrets, either, not at this unholy intersection of anomie and big-time news. The story's been taken away from him and other people are now trying to affect the plot. The police have a story they'd like to tell and so do the media folks and so, I suppose, do I, although in the hierarchy of things I suspect I'm just as clueless as the Bad Guy. When I arrive at First and Vine he's busy negotiating by phone. He wants to know what kind of trouble he's in.

The falling rain makes a pleasant hum on the asphalt but barely a block away the whole city gives out, dissolved in a granular fog, and I dreamily sense that out there, out beyond the end of the avenues and streets where right now the only destination I see is murk, there might be silence again, a silence we might enter and lose ourselves in and thereby forget all this cowboy business of guns and women. Meanwhile back in the real world my first instinct is a sort of stupid ducking motion I've learned from the movies, and I have the sure sense I'm going to be shot in the neck, where I feel particularly exposed and vulnerable. At first I don't know in which building the guy's holed up, and I assume it's one of the high-rise Miami Beach-style architectural monstrosities that distort the human scale of this, the north end of Belltown. But this assumption is just pure cornball stuff, and I'm instantly aware that everything I feel and think is little more than the coalescence of certain clichés, that the Bad Guy isn't a madman barricaded in the top floor of the tallest building, that he doesn't necessarily plan to take potshots at pedestrians and commuters on their way to work, that he might just be drunk and deranged and wondering how he came to this strange pass on an ordinary evening that began normally enough and is now in the wee hours rapidly going to hell. In short, I don't know anything about him, beginning with the most fundamental thing, like where he is.

Not knowing where he is translates pretty soon into a polymorphous fear, and now it's not just my neck constricting, but also my shoulders and my stomach and my balls, the fear having spread practically right down to my toes as I vividly imagine all the places a bullet can enter the body, and I try to squat casually—casually because I don't want to embarrass myself in front of the gathering pack of seasoned hardcore TV news journalists, who frankly seem, with all their unwieldy equipment and their lackadaisical milling around, like sitting ducks—behind a cement wall until it occurs to me that the whole notion of being "behind" anything is a logistical matter I can't quite coordinate, since I don't know where the Bad Guy is. A ballistic line from point A (Bad Guy) to point B (author's neck) can't be established just yet, and for all I know I might actually be casually squatting right in front of him, cleanly fixed between his sights. In deer and elk hunting there's a moment when you sight your quarry, when everything is there, and you feel the weighty potential of the imminent second in your every nerve, and this weight, this sense of anticipation, this prolepsis, can really screw up your shot. It's as if the moment were vibrating, taking on static interference from the past and the future, and success depends on your ability to still it, to calm yourself through careful breathing right back into the singular present. Variously called buck or bull fever, I'm now feeling a variant of that, imagining myself notched neatly in the iron sights of the Bad Guy's gun. My fear is as vaporous and real and enveloping as the rain and fog and I have this not-unfamiliar feeling of general and impending doom.

This might seem unnecessarily preambular, but I also want to say my pants are falling down and I'm sopping wet. I came back from salmon fishing in Alaska with a severe case of atopic dermatitis primarily caused by contact with neoprene. I had what's called an "id" reaction—pretty much systemic—and all week my fingers and neck and feet and legs were puffy and disgusting with weeping sores. I think my condition even freaked the dermatologist. My hands were so raw and inflamed I wasn't able to type, hold a pen, or turn the pages of a book. Because I don't own a television, my week of forced zombiism passed without distraction and nothing to gnaw on but my own increasingly desperate thoughts. I lay in bed, staring at the ceiling, the walls. It was a new kind of aloneness for me, being imprisoned in my own skin. It was easy to imagine never being touched by another human being ever again. The dermatitis made my skin crawl and I was taking 40 mg of prednisone, a steroid that cruelly kept me awake so as, it seemed, to fully and consciously experience my suffering in a state of maximum alertness. I mention all this to establish a certain oblique connective tissue between observer and observed, between myself as witness and the thing witnessed. Half the reason I'm at the crime scene is I haven't had any human contact for a while and besides I can't sleep with my skin prickling (and the other half of why I'm standing in the rain at two in the morning is I'm probably some kind of tragedy pervert). When I got back from Alaska my hands were already painfully suppurating and I couldn't carry all my bags and only grabbed the expensive stuff, the rods and reels, leaving a duffle of clothes in my truck. The next time I could put shoes on and walk, three days later, the neighborhood crackheads had stolen my clothes, including my only belt and my only raincoat, and that's why my drawers droop and I'm soaked and starting to shiver a little in this melissonant humming rain.

But I didn't come to this crime-scene-in-progress innocently. Before leaving the apartment I put a pen in my pocket, along with a stack of 3 x 5 cards and a tape recorder, thinking that if this thing got real hairy, if there was actually some shooting, then I might jot a few notes and make of an otherwise blank night a bonafide journalistic story, full of who, what, where, when. Like a lot of my aspirations this one, too, was internally doomed and hopeless long before I realized it. My main problem vis-à-vis journalism is I just don't have an instinct for what's important. I realize that now, looking over my notes. My first note was about the old alleys in Seattle, those island places where stickerbushes flourish and a man can still sleep on a patch of bare earth, where paths are worn like game trails and leave a trace of people's passing, and how these naturally surviving spots are systematically vanishing from the city, rooted up and paved over mostly because they house bums— an act of eradication that seems as emotionally mingy as putting pay slots on public toilets but is probably cost-effective in terms of maintenance, since bums generate a lot of garbage in the form of broken glass and hot dog wrappers and wet cardboard. Then I started another note about how, in contrast to these hardscrabble plots, the flower beds and parking strips of lush grass and manicured shrubs and trees are pampered and how, currently, it's like three in the morning and all up and down the street automatic sprinklers spit and hiss in the rain, redundantly watering.

Also my notes bleed black ink and blur and vanish in the rain as I write them. I don't write a note about that.

But after investigating the alley it occurs to me there's a whole parking lot full of highly paid professional journalists just loafing around and that some of them might answer a few questions. I'm not properly credentialed and I'm feeling a little timid because, with my falling-down pants, my soaking-wet waxed-cotton coat, and my sore, swollen, hideous, raw red fingers, I don't look nearly so crisp and ready to report news as these people, and in fact, the way I look, I might be an escapee from the other side, I might just *be* a piece of news myself, but I need to approach them and find out what's going on and, if nothing else, I'd really like to fix on a location for the Bad Guy. Certainly these journalists know the scoop, otherwise they wouldn't look nearly so bored and unconcerned. Watching them from a distance, I have the feeling we're all waiting for dawn and that dawn, in turn, will bring us death; the atmosphere is straight out of an old Western, where the man gets hanged at sunup. I mean this whole aimless scene badly needs a plot, and nothing emphasizes that more than these journalists, these TV people, standing around in a parking lot scattered with expensive equipment that now waits idly for . . . *something*. All this inaction is underscored and made emphatic by the sheer number of journalists flocking in the lot, which creates a sense of collective antic-ipation, a weird hope. Really it would be a relief if that gun would go off.

In a kind of illustrated food chain of journalism there are big white vans representing every major TV station in Seattle and then several shrimpy economy cars, also white, with the names of radio stations printed on the doors. I notice every journalist is wearing a particularly nice rain-coat, with team colors. Then I notice other things, like the cameras, the monitors; they too are covered in specially made rain bonnets. And a couple people are walking around with umbrellas the size of parachutes. All these dry people are like from another tribe. This kind of hard-hitting high-level journalism obviously requires neat hair, which partly explains all the first-rate raingear, and that equipment can't be cheap, not like 3 x 5 cards. One of the TV reporters is wearing navy blue pants and a red coat, an outfit that resembles the unsexed uniform of a reservations clerk for a national hotel chain. Another TV guy is practicing a look of grave concern in his monitor, a look that, live at least, seems woefully constipated. It's weird to watch what amounts oxymoronically to a rehearsal of urgent news, especially without sound, emptied of content, because this pantomime of immediacy is patently fake, a charade, a fine-tuning, not of emotions, but the reenacted look of emotions. It's method acting or something. In a curious twist, I realize I always knew TV news *seemed* full of shit, but I never knew it was, in fact, full of shit. Previously I thought the TV news had a certain endemic phoniness because all the reporters were sorority girls who'd majored in communications, but it never occurred to me that the fakery was intentional. These people do this on purpose, and realizing that stunned me, because all my life I'd generously overlooked the canned quality of broadcast journalism, thinking it was, like other infirmities, something these people couldn't help. I thought they were just naturally corny people and no more deserving of scorn than cripples, and in fact were entitled, because of their impairment, to an extra helping of tolerance and understanding on my part. And now this morning I'm learning that that peculiar phony quality really is phony.

It's all big-time wrestling.

It occurs to me I'm not supple enough of an ironist to be alive and freely moving around in public anymore. With my skin practically leprous I might just hang a cowbell off my neck and clang around town the rest of my days.

I'm not going to mention the name of the big-league TV journalist I finally talked to because later in the morning, in between taping the twenty-five seconds of filler that feeds into the national show, he tried on a couple occasions to pick up secretaries who'd come out on the sidewalk to gawk. Every time I turned around he was chatting up another secretary, then he'd rush in front of the camera and morph into the face of a slightly panicked and alarmed person nevertheless manfully maintaining heroic control while reporting nearby horrors. To look at his on-camera face you'd think Godzilla was eating lawyers off the Winslow ferry. It was clear to me that sometime in the past the putative luster of his job had landed him in bed with bystanders.

But before that, I thought he might be a reliable source of information.

"Hey," I said, "what do you think of this?"

"It's wet," the guy said, and then, I kid you not, he lit up a cigarette, and squinted at the sky—just like a hero of some sort.

In a study of poetics you'd call that kind of rhetorical understatement meiosis. In its most simple metalogical form it works by deadpanning the ostensive situation (the Bad Guy with the gun, the hostage, homicidal intent) by rerouting it through the bluntly obvious and uninteresting observation that it is raining. This kind of locution can be found in *King Lear* and some of Auden's poetry and it's nearly a national mental disease in England, plus it's pretty common in war, where the irony functions as an anodyne against other, more painful emotions.

Putting moves on secretaries, phony-faced reports, meiosis—you can't finally penetrate the pose to anything real.

I walk off and get my story by eavesdropping on a wondrously cute black woman wearing a blue coat, the back of which quite clearly states, in reflective block letters, her purpose: Seattle Police Media Relations. She's exactly what I've been looking for, maybe all my life. She's the unambiguous source of everybody else's story anyway. The most interesting thing I learn is there's no hostage.

"Is there a reporter here?" some guy demands to know.

His voice wavers with anger but his question floats unanswered and hangs ignored in a rude silence until, unnerved, I point to the parking lot and say, "Yeah, there's tons of them. They're all over the place."

Even as I watch the guy walk off I know in a low-frequency animal-to-animal way he's the one, the man I need to talk to. Some part of this story is lodged inside him. In terms of clothing alone he's way worse off than me, and what he's wearing, jeans and a T-shirt, shows he's been rudely expelled from one cozy circumstance and dragged against his will into the rain. He's now caught in between, trapped in some place I recognize as life itself. It's obvious he hasn't been sober in hours and maybe years. If it could be said that these big-deal journalists have control of the story, and therefore, in a fundamental sense, are liars, albeit professional and highly compensated, then this guy is the antijournalist, because in his case the story is steering him, shoving him around and blowing him willy-nilly down the street. The truth is just fucking with him and he's suffering narrative problems. He began the night with no intention of standing in this rain and his exposure to it is pitiful. As he moves unheeded like the Ancient Mariner through the journalists I feel a certain brotherly sympathy for him and I'm enamored of his utter lack of dignity. He's moved beyond all poses. I know he'll come back to me, that it's just a matter of a little more rejection, and when he returns, when he settles on me, I'll welcome him like a prodigal.

He doesn't know it yet, but I'll listen to him.

Meanwhile we're at the edge of dawn, a first feathering

of gray light that brings a bum stampede to the streets of Belltown. I live down here, and every morning at roughly five o'clock bums pour out of the missions and shelters and alleys in a kind of shabby and shadowy pre-commute, followed by the real thing an hour or two later. They pool up and briefly form a chorus. They fish around in squashed packs of GPC cigarettes, fire up. "Look at these news-media dicks," they say. Lights have come on in the IBEW Local 46 building and a few guys with lunch-buckets are standing outside the Labor Temple Restaurant and Lounge. More and more people are standing around, trying to figure out what's going on. When the bums ask what's happening the question sounds yearningly metaphysical or like a child stirring from a dream. Their need to know, at any rate, is tonally different than that of a big-league journalist. And still we've got beaucoup reporters doing their insane pantomime of sincerity in the parking lot. It's like the Hitler tryouts in that Mel Brooks movie *The Producers*. None of the TV people have budged from their encampment in the parking lot, and I realize they're operating under the strictest criterion of relevance—every camera is focused in the same direction—and that their sense of the narrative is, generally, in sync with the police, that is, their reason for being here will end in a roughly coincident moment.

The guy's back. No one will listen to him, he's just learned.

"These fucking cops," he starts right up. "These god-damn pigs! They said there's no room on the bus. Me and my friend been standing in the rain all night. I'm a vet and he's an American Native. That ain't right. And these fuck-ing assholes—you don't believe me? Here's my card."

He shows me his veterans ID, establishing his credentials, his suprapatriotic right to feel and also express his grievous outrage.

"That's some real shit," he says. "Dennis R. Burns. US Army Retired."

I tell him my first name.

"You know anybody?" he asks.

"You mean, like, somebody that could do something? Like Jesus Christ?"

"You a Born Again?"

"I was just joking."

"I know somebody," Dennis says.

I ask him if he knows what's going on.

"Yeah, got a guy with a gun, big black guy, 110 Vine Street, apartment #210. L. was throwing furniture at his girlfriend. This was about midnight. I'm the one that called the police, stupid me. I'm the maintenance man. L.'s generally a quiet guy, a little hypertensive, but nice. Very intelligent, well spoken."

"So he has a gun?"

"He's got two, a .9MM and something else, like a .357. I hope they don't hurt the man. Are you a journalist?"

"I'm really wet. You want some coffee?"

"What happened to your hands?"

"They're all fucked up. It's not contagious or anything."

"Are you a reporter?"

"Yeah," I say.

"7-Eleven's open. We could get coffee at 7-Eleven."

On the way there I pull out my Olympus Pearlcorder s803—testing, one, two, three—and discover the batteries are dead.

"You sure you're a journalist?" Dennis says. "Hey, my son's an editorial cartoonist for the *Albuquerque Times*. He makes fun of everything—politicians, everything. He's always got a shitty fucking look on his face—like you."

On the way back from 7-Eleven with our coffees we hook up with Tom, who's drinking something throttled in a brown bag. He tells me, "I been up all night and I'm getting kinda moody. We were just gonna get drunk and listen to Elton John or some Asian music. But this gunman kept me up all night."

"And they wouldn't let us on the bus," Dennis says. And then he asks, "You ever write about Veteran's Affairs?"

I feel bad I've led him on. "No," I say.

"There's prejudice on the bus," Tom says. "Those that like to drink and raise hell can't get on the bus. I tried to sleep on the sidewalk but it didn't feel right."

I ask about the gunman again.

Tom says, "I don't like L. but he's a human being. I live right above him and he's always yelling, 'I don't like white music!' I'm reservation Indian, but I'm part white too. I'm glad he's gone. He's gone now. He's not a tenant. Soon as he gives up, I mean."

I really want to know who the gunman is but certain elements of life in what's essentially an SRO conspire against the ready flow of this kind of information. In the main you're talking about people at the tail end of a trajectory, people who aren't any longer carrying around much of the baggage by which we're known to each other, family, jobs, schools, common aspirations, sundry memberships and affiliations, political grievances, etc., and so asking for anything in the way of remotely biographical material brings scarcely more than vagaries. Dennis, for instance, insisted several times that the Bad Guy, L., was nice, a nice guy—but I don't get what kind of very elastic notion of "nice" he's talking about, given what's going on. And while of course everyone, even the most wrecked and destitute among us, has a unique personal history, the problematic nature of trying to gather information about people who've severed too many basic ties is this, that in a sense we truly have history only insofar as it's shared and too much uniqueness really leads away from individuality to anonymity, the great sea of the forgotten. And because the Bad Guy is busy and I can't talk to him, I've got to rely on people who might reasonably be expected to know him, and in fact don't. I suppose it could also be said we're known to the extent that we're dull and orbital about our life, that what's quotidian about us is more easily shared than the exuberances and passions that push us out of the predictable.

And something like this is further confirmed when Dennis, Tom, and I arrive at the bus. Apparently the deal is that Metro brings around a bus for all the folks who've been forced to evacuate in situations like this, an ordinary accordion-style city bus where people can sleep and keep warm. Inside this bus what you see is pretty much a jackpot of social and psychic collapse, a demographic of bad news. Everybody in there's fucked-up in some heavy way, dragged out of history by alcohol, drugs, mental illness, physical decrepitude, crime, old age, poverty, whatever. Riding this bus in your dreams would give you the heebie-jeebies big-time. There are maybe ten or fifteen people on the bus but between them if you counted you'd probably only come up with sixty teeth. In addition to dental trouble, there're people leaning on canes, people twitching and barefoot with yellow toenails curled like talons, gray-skinned people shivering in gauzy nightgowns, others who just tremble and stare. They've been ripped out of their bedrooms and are dressed mostly in nightwear, which is something to see—not because I have any fashion ideas or big thesis about nighties and pj's, but rather because, this surreal dawn, the harsh isolated privacy of these people is literally being paraded in public. The falling rain, the bus going nowhere, the wrecked-up passengers dressed for sleep, the man with the gun—these are the wild and disparate components of a dream, and I haven't slept, and it's just weird.

And meantime that rodentlike anti-whatever vehicle has parked in the street below the Bad Guy's window and there's a super highly trained SWAT-type guy launching tear gas canisters. We hear the dull pop report like a distant shotgun blast, and then a rainy sprinkling of broken glass on the sidewalk.

"There go the windows," Dennis says. "Those are double-pane, $145 a piece. I got a very secure job."

"Look how fast I left," Tom says. He pulls a TV remote control out of the pocket of his sweats and clicks at the sky. "It's pitiful, I know. It's pitiful."

"What are the rooms like?" I ask, kind of trying to figure the size of the rooms and calculate how fast the pepper spray or tear gas or whatever will take effect.

Dennis says, "You got one room. You got a stove in the room. You got a fridge in the room. You got a bed."

After hearing Dennis describe the Bad Guy's room, the story, the night, everything, starts to end for me. I know they haven't got him and maybe things'll go crazy an hour from now, two hours from now, and people will die or some other TVish sort of scenario will play itself out, but I don't care. I've been out here for seven plus hours and I'm really wet and can't hardly bend my fingers anymore. My feet ache and swell inside my boots, even though I've removed the laces. But that room! I'm starting to feel all buggy imagining that man in that room. It sounds so simple, so stripped, so precariously close to nothing, yet outside all this complication is whirling around, cops and meter maids and a SWAT guy and a crisis negotiator and TV and spectators, everyone focused on this man in a room with a stove, a fridge, and a bed.

What would you do? How would you end this story?

I walk back to my place, change into dry pants and feed the dog a bowl of kibble. I sit on the edge of my bed. To keep my feet from cracking I've bought a lot of fancy lotions, the labels of which make outlandish, existential promises. One offers itself as "cruelty-free"; another says it will rid my skin of the toxins that are an inescapable part of modern life. The thing is, over the last couple weeks my desire to believe has collapsed into actual belief, and I slather the stuff on like holy water at Lourdes.

I ease my feet into my boots and head back to First and Vine. In my mind I'm turning over the possibility that this whole strange night is a love story, and that if it is, if in fact there's some kind of romance at the heart of it all, then the entire event will elude me. Also I wonder, in an idle, academic way, why the police alone are so refreshingly without irony. Then I wonder why I find it refreshing. Then I think about the crackheads who stole my belt and raincoat and how the economics of addiction might connect up with this event. Then I go back to considering the love angle, how it's nearly impossible to convey our deepest passions yet damned easy to share what's dullest and worst about ourselves. I'm already composing the story in my head, but when I get back to First and Vine everyone's gone. The crime scene is no longer officially a scene because the yellow ribbon has been rolled up and taken away. The Bad Guy has surrendered. The police have left. The TV people are off on other assignments. Dennis is gone. Tom is gone. The bus is gone. The window is bashed to hell, the blinds mangled, but otherwise there's no sign of the siege and the night's dreamy drama; the workaday world is beginning and all of life is back to pumpkins and mice, and I feel like I'm just waking up, standing there on the sidewalk, all alone, loitering.

Seattle, 1974

The initial salvos in my hankering to expatriate took the predictable route of firing snobby potshots at the local icons of culture, at Ivar with his hokey ukelele and Stan Boreson and Dick Balsch with his ten-pound sledge bashing cars and laughing like a maniac all through the late night, etc. (Actually I thought DB was cool and so did a good many of my friends. He had the crude sinister good looks of a porn star and once merited an admiring squib in *Time.* In his cheap improvised commercials—interrupting roller derby and the antics of Joannie Weston, "the Blonde Amazon"—he'd beat brand-new cars with a hammer, so to me he always seemed superior to circumstance—our old cars just got beat to hell by life, whereas Dick Balsch went out on the attack. It was a period when a lot of us hero-worshipped people who destroyed things and even now I wonder where DB's gone and half hope he'll come back and smash more stuff.) Anyone born in geographical exile, anyone from the provinces, anyone for whom the movements of culture feel rumored, anyone like this grows up anxiously aware that all the innovative and vital events in the world happen Back East, like way back, like probably France, but before expatriation can be accomplished in fact it is rehearsed and performed in the head. You make yourself clever and scoffing, ironic, deracinated, cold and quick to despise. You import your enthusiasms from the past, other languages, traditions. You make the voyage first in the aisles of bookstores and libraries, in your feckless dreams. The books you love best feature people who ditched their homes in the hinterlands for scenes of richer glory. Pretty soon the word *Paris* takes on a numinous quality and you know you won't be silent forever. Someday you'll leave.

Meanwhile, the only city I really knew was a dump worse than anything Julius Pierpont Patches (local TV clown) ever dreamed of, sunk in depression and completely off the cultural map, no matter what outlandish claims local boosters made for the region. And they made many. In a highly cherished book of mine (*You Can't Eat Mount Rainier*, by William Speidel Jr., Bob Cram illustrator, © 1955) I read, "What with the city's leading professional men, artists, writers, world travelers and visiting VIPs always dropping into the place, (Ivar's) has become the spot where clams and culture meet." Huh? Artists? Writers? To explain, Ivar's is a local seafood restaurant and Ivar himself was a failed folksinger in the tradition of the

Weavers. Back then there was an abundance of clams and a paucity of culture, but even more than this disparity, I'd somehow arranged it in my head that clams, salmon, steelhead, and geoducks were actually antithetical to and the sworn enemies of culture. No one wrote about them, is what I probably meant. Perhaps clams and culture met, once, in 1955, but then of course 1955 stubbornly persisted in Seattle until like 1980, and in between time you felt stuck mostly with mollusks. The culture side of the equation was most prominently represented by a handful of aging rear guard cornballs. Like Ivar himself.

If you were a certain type, and I was, you first had to dismantle the local scene's paltry offerings and then build up in its place a personal pantheon remote from the very notion that clams and culture really ever do meet, anywhere, at a time when, all arrogant and hostile and a budding prig, you believed culture was the proprietary right of a few Parisians. That an old warbly voiced yokel like Ivar might pass for culture, or that *Here Come the Brides* might signify to the world your sense of place, seemed a horror, an embarrassment. I went incognito, I developed alibis. For starters I took to wearing a black Basque beret and became otherwise ludicrously Francophile in my tastes. Mostly, however, I couldn't find solid purchase for my *snobisme*. Not that I didn't try. I'd have liked to be some old hincty Henry James but couldn't really sustain it. Still you badly wanted things delocalized, just a little. Even if you had to do it first just in your head, with issueless irony. You looked about. With a skeptical eye you sized up the offerings. You wondered, for instance, why it was that suddenly in Seattle there was an aesthetic love of statues. You wondered, what is it with all these replicas of people around the region? A brass Ivar and his brass seagulls, some apparently homeless people (brass) in the courtyard of the Sedgwick James Bldg. (as if a real, non-brass loiterer could actually rest awhile on those benches unmolested), and then, last, least, a hideous band of five or six citizens (cement) waiting for the bus in Fremont. Like a bunch of gargoyles walked off their ancient job guttering rain, they've been waiting for the bus twenty or thirty years now. If you've lived here long enough (like a week) you know the rain of today is the rain of tomorrow and the rain of a million years ago and if you stand in that eternal rain long enough and often enough you start to feel replicating the experience rubs it in your face. I've stood in the rain and waited for buses or whatever and it wasn't a joke, not that I understood, at least. You're standing there, you're buzzed, you're bored, you're waiting, you don't have a schedule, the rain's pounding around your head like nuthouse jibberjabber, and from this incessant and everlasting misery someone else works up an instance of passing cleverness, then casts it in concrete for all time?

Those stone citizens, silent and forever waiting, are like my nightmare.

———

I badly wanted to escape my unwritten city for a time and place already developed by words, for Paris or London or Berlin and a particular epoch as it existed in books. I wanted Culture, the uppercase sort. Books fit my minimum-wage budget and afforded the cheapest access. Fifty cents bought admission to the best. I purchased most of my early novels and poems from a woman who, I recall, only had one leg. Later there was Elliott Bay Book Company, which offered both a bookstore and a brick-walled garret in the basement. You could loiter without having to skulk. You could bring your empty cup to the register and ask for refills. And you could read. Those books, more than any plane ticket, offered a way out. Admittedly it was a lonely prescription, an Rx that might better have been replaced by 100 mg of whatever tricyclate was cutting-edge back in the seventies. But who knew about such things? Instead I'd hide out in the basement of Elliott Bay or in the top floor of the Athenian and in my sporadic blue notebooks track a reading list—Joyce, Pound, Eliot, et al.—that was really little more than a syllabus for a course on exile. You could probably dismiss this as one of those charming agonies of late adolescence, but let me suggest that it's also a logical first step in developing an aesthetic, a reach toward historical beauty, the desire to join yourself to what's already been appreciated and admired. You want to find yourself in the flow of time, miraculously relieved of your irrelevance. For reasons both sensible and suspect folks today are uneasy with the idea of a tradition, but the intellectual luxury of this stance wasn't available to me, and I saw the pursuit of historical beauty, the yearning for those higher essences other people had staked their lives on, as the hope for some kind of voice, a chance to join the chorus. I was mad for relevance, connection, some hint that I was not alone. I started scribbling in notebooks in part just so I'd have an excuse, a reason for sitting where I sat, an alibi for being by myself.

Seattle in the seventies was the nadir of just everything. A University of Washington prof of mine, a yam-faced veteran of SDS, inelegantly labeled us "the phlegmatic generation." The word *apathy* got used an awful lot. I quite sincerely believe Karen Ann Quinlan was the decade's sex symbol. Seeking an alchemic dullness in quaaludes and alcohol, she actually found apotheosis in a coma; that's what made her so sexy (i.e., compelling) and symbolic to me. I'm not trying to be ironic or waggish here. Objects restore a measure of silence to the world, and she was, for those ten wordless years, an object. Her speechless plight seemed resonant, delphic. The reason I remember her as such an emblematic figure is her coma coincided with my own incognizant youth. The Seattle of that time had a distinctly comalike aspect and at night seemed to contain in its great sleepy volume precisely one of everything, one dog a-barking, one car a-cranking, one door a-slamming, etc., and then an extravagant, unnecessary amount of nothing. Beaucoup nothing. The kind of expansive, hardly differentiated, foggy and final nothing you imagine a coma induces. I read the silence as a kind of Nordic parsimony. An act of middle-class thrift. A soporific seeded into the clouds. All the decent dull blockheads were asleep, and you could no more wake them to vivid life than you could KAQ. Being alone at night in Seattle began to seem horrifying, there was just so much nothing and so little of me.

You know how the story goes—I went away, I came back, blah blah. I now see the personal element in all this, the comic note, and I also realize the high European graft doesn't readily take to all American subjects. The predominant mental outlook of people I grew up with depended largely on a gargantuan isolation. When I finally went away I was always careful to tell people I was from Seattle, *Washington*, afraid they wouldn't know where the city was, which suggests the isolation of the place was permanently lodged in me. Finding myself at last in the warm heart of culture, in New York or Paris or even L.A., I returned, like some kind of revanchist, to the cold silent topography I knew best, the landscape of my hurt soul. I first read Raymond Carver because in paging through his second collection at a bookstore I noticed a familiar place-name— Wenatchee—and latched onto the work solely based on that simple recognition. Ditto Ken Kesey. And then there was the discovery of Richard Hugo, a great epic namer, who beautifully described himself as "a wrong thing in a right world," and noted the oppressive quiet of the city the way I had, so that it seemed we were brothers, and offered to me a liberating emblem far better suited to my ambitions as a writer than a girl in a coma. These are probably just the humdrum dilemmas any writer encounters, and that I should express any keen pain at the difficulty of finding a subject and a voice is, I realize, kind of carping and obnoxious. It comes with the territory, after all.

And yet it is still some form of familiar silence that I struggle against when I write, something essential about the isolation. As Graham Greene wrote: "At that age one may fall irrevocably in love with failure, and success of any kind loses half its savour before it is experienced." For me the city is still inarticulate and dark and a place I call home because I'm in thrall to failure and to silence—I have a fidelity to it, an allegiance, which presents a strange dislocation now that Seattle's become the Valhalla of so many people's seeking. The idea of it as a locus of economic and scenic and cultural hope baffles me. It a little bit shocks me to realize my nephews and nieces are growing up in a place considered desirable. That will be their idea, rightly. That wasn't my idea at all. Vaguely groping for a diluted tertiary memory, people used to say to me, I've heard it's nice *out there,* and I'd say, Seattle has a really high suicide rate. (I was kind of an awkward conversationalist.) But really I didn't know if it was nice; it never occurred to me to wonder. I'd shyly shrug and mumble out of the conversation, saying I didn't know, it was home. Seattle does have a suicide rate a couple notches above the national average and so does my family and I guess that earns me the colors of some kind of native. I walk around, I try to check it out, this new world of hope and the good life, but in some part of my head it's forever 1974 and raining and I'm a kid and a man with a shopping cart full of kiped meat clatters down the sidewalk chased with sad enthusiasm by apron-wearing box boys who are really full-grown men recently pink-slipped at Boeing and now scabbing part-time at Safeway.

Today I go in search of an older city, a silent city. Early in the morning the painted signs on the buildings downtown seem to rise away from the brick in a kind of layered pentimento. The light at that hour comes at a certain angle and is gentle and noticeably slower and words gradually emerge from the walls. *Your Credit Is Good. The Best In Raingear.* There is a place I can stand on Westlake Avenue and read the fading signs and recognize many of the names of people I grew up with. I've got my own people buried in the ground. I cross the Aurora Bridge and think special thoughts and know my brother's black Wellingtons are buried in the shifting toxic silt at the bottom of Lake Union. That brother's alive, and I thank god for certain kinds of failure. New silences layer over the old. I hope this brief superficial essay hasn't simply circled around a peculiar woundedness. Folks double my age and older often run down a conversation tracking a vanishing world that will, with the passing of their memory, vanish entirely. This is something more than benign senescent forgetfulness. So be it. Nowadays I feel like an old-timer in terms of estrangement. I don't know what determines meaning in the city any better than these old people with their attenuating memories. Probably traffic laws, the way we still agree to agree on the denotation of stop signs. I went away and in my absence other things have sprung up. Good things. It's a new place, but there's an old silence bothering me.

And now when I write I feel the silence pressuring the words just like the silence I felt as a kid, walking around town, with nowhere to go. It used to be I'd wander down the alley around the corner from the Yankee Peddler and see if Floyd the Flowerman was in his shack. Floyd sold flowers out of a homemade shack, a lean-to patched together out of realtor's sandwich boards and such and propped up against what's now a soap shop, and he was a big fan of police scanners, of the mysteries of other people's misfortunes as they cackled over the airwaves and received, at least briefly, a specific locus, a definite coordinate within the city. This oddball interest in fixing the detailed location of pain and disaster fascinated me. I'd say it prefigured the job of a writer, if the conceit weren't so obviously tidy. I can't now tell if Floyd was crazy. Probably he was just sixties jetsam, tossed overboard by the era and living like a kind of alleycat Brautigan "made lonely and strange by that Pacific Northwest of so many years ago, that dark rainy land . . ." That wet black alley, and then the queer miracle of his white shack, those floodlit plasterbuckets filled with red gladiolus, sunflowers, pink carnations, and then Floyd the hippie holdover tuning his scanner into instances of tragedy, dialing up meaning and its shifting vectors. One night when the bus just wouldn't come Floyd and I walked in the rain down Stone Way to watch a house burn. He was very hepped up. The cold rain on our faces warmed to tear-temperature in the heat of the burning house. I wish time would collapse so I could be watching flames and ash rise from that house and also see my brother falling through the air below the bridge. Obscurely I know this is a wish that Time, like a god, might visit us all in our moment of need. But Floyd's gone and that brother's got a metal plate in his pelvis and walks a little funny and myself, I wander around at night, taking long walks to clear my head before sitting down in front of my type-writer, walking for an hour or two as all the new and desirable good floats before me like things in a dream, out of reach, and I peer through the windows of new restaurants and new shops and see all the new people but I don't go in, probably because I feel more in my element as the man who is out there standing in the rain or just passing by on his way home to write.

Mary Kay Letourneau

The King County Regional Justice Center is a kind of justice multiplex and includes under one roof a jail, courts, probation stuff, covered parking, all the amenities. Outside the parking garage on a patch of sloping lawn there's a sculpture garden with a NATIVE AMERICAN motif—big trinkets of rebar bent to look like tepees, arrows, some kind of mandala/dreamcatcher thing, a piscine shape, etc. Looking at it you feel less in the elevated presence of art than hammered over the head by a governmental or bureaucratic intention and the effect is of sovietized realism, of culture that's policed, official, approved, frozen, cliché, one-note, panderly, in other words, everything that art is not.

Winding past this display of agitprop is a path lined with lampposts whose fixtures are a kitsch rendition of the scales of justice. That path leads to a glass door with an ingenious pneumatic device that replicates good manners by holding the door open for you and, after a polite interval perfectly timed to let you in, shutting it quietly behind you, and once inside you find a seamless continuation of the same orthodox themes, the same didacticism, the same blunt clarity of signs, as in the bush art outside. Just about everywhere you turn there's a placard that tells you what to do or not do. The hallways are full of instruction. Your behavior's directed. Press to Open. No Smoking. No Weapons Allowed. No guns, no knives, no chemical sprays, etc. For Public Safety the use of skateboards roller skates roller blades Strictly Prohibited. Please use revolving doors. Eviction info in rm 1B/1100. Men. Women. (Generic bathroom symbols, with gender distinguished by skirt (girls), pants (boys).) You feel squeezed by subtext, monitored like a child in class, but you also wonder a little what evil alien race of cartoon figures comes here in need of so much explicit guidance. Probably a lot of the people entering the RJC have demonstrated an impaired ability to read the signs out in society and maybe that explains the need for Mosaic clarity. The signs steer the stream of prevaricators in the right direction for once.

In a windowed rotunda there's a guy with a red feather duster dusting away at 7 AM. He doesn't seem to come by dusting naturally, there's a dispirited VoTech or Occupational Therapy aspect to the way he does the job, a trained make-work quality, a lack of flair, especially when he starts dusting the walls. The walls! I keep watching and wondering what dust has fallen on this immaculate place in the night. It looks like he's trying to catch the dust in flight, before it lands. Preventive dusting. I watch him wave the duster and I listen to the shoptalk of journalists. It sounds really important having this proximal relation to reality, to live every day of your life as the next-door neighbor to the truth. After a while the courtroom opens and the big fish in the media pool are ushered in and seated so they'll get the clearest view (camera angle) of Mary Kay Letourneau when the time comes. Myself, I'm seated right behind the family of the young man I'll call X and who for dramatic purposes the press has labeled a boy or a child or a victim. When Letourneau enters stage left and sits beside her lawyer I have an obstructed view of the back of her head. At my age I've seen the backs of untold thousands of heads—more backs than fronts, probably—and note nothing particularly interesting to say about hers.

Mary Kay Letourneau dared to be unclear in public. "I wish," she said, "there was a story that made sense and could be told right now, but there isn't." When she arrived in court for the sentencing she had a frail wispy etiolated look from having spent months in jail but otherwise her in-person face showed the same smudged and incoherent prettiness captured in countless pictures. I'd seen plenty of those photos in the papers and magazines and with each instance I wondered why her features weren't in focus. But it turns out they were, it's just that her face, even in real life, appears clouded and dreamy and somewhat removed from the immediate scene. Her lawyer David Gerhke characterized her as a woman with "a screw loose" who "doesn't know how to separate reality and fantasy." Her husband, Steve Letourneau, for some ulterior reason wanted everybody to know she was not Mary Poppins. In my experience the strategy a lot of frightened women turn to is that of making themselves intangible. Rather than go hard and confrontational the way a man in crisis might, they become ethereal and really remote. Based on no one's authority but my own, I would say Letourneau showed the mien of a battered woman, of someone in retreat from her own face, whose safe haven is inward, reclusive, so-litary, distant, and that what you saw in the pictures, in the photographed face the press captioned variously as belonging in an abstract allegoric uppercase way to a Wife, a Teacher, a Mother, was little more than a mask she'd vacated a long time ago.

She wasn't clear. She insisted until she was silenced by Lawyer Gerhke and pressured by the public call for a kowtowing show of remorse and civic obedience that her relationship with X was love. She said that "given the nature of this situation—and that includes the charges against me, the media, everything—there isn't anything *within legal bounds* that I can say to help make sense of what is happening." (My italics.) Against the chorus of experts who in one rote voice claimed her relationship with X was "distortion" and "manipulation" and "rationalization," Letourneau said, "I would not expect people to understand, but it did exist and it was real." She was never loose or gallionic about the gravity of her situation and her public statements always struck me as honest and unfiltered, a too-frank, badly lawyered expression of confusion that rang true, not because she was successful in justifying or rationalizing her actions, but precisely because she was hesitant, uncertain, floundering—precisely because she failed, and failed publicly! She never told us what we wanted to hear. She wasn't glib, she wasn't corny, she never once deliberately lied or even delivered a pat, practiced answer. Given the boundaries she'd crossed and the taboos she'd broken and the generally undone state of her life it's incredible to me she was able to speak at all. The story drew prurient attention locally and from around the country, and soon after that the experts moved in with their Extra-Strength vocabularies, the proficient idioms of the law, of social work, of psychology, but Letourneau alone seemed to have trouble finding words. You could hear in her voice and in the absence of cant that her true feelings, whatever they were, like Cordelia's love, were more ponderous than her tongue.

———

Pretty much the opposite of Letourneau's hesitance was the insta-commentary offered up by local broadcasters. After the sentencing one Bonnie Hart from KIRO or KOMO—I forget which and don't believe it really matters—quickly convened a kind of radio Sanhedrin. As far as I know BH's only real qualification for commenting on Letourneau is that she holds a job that requires her to say something re: something most every day of the week. Day after day I suppose she's paid to be fluent in politics, cookbooks, fresh vegetables, fads, open or closed batting stances, menopause, studded tires, whatever. In other words, her authority is mostly occupational, though it seems she's possessed of omniscience. Her opinions weren't suasive enough to win me over, not by any of the common measures I developed as a Catholic kid avidly listening for lame moments in hundreds of homilies. No elegance or force of thought, no wit, no keen insight, no revelatory moments that broadened perspectives, that enlivened feelings, no resonance, no self-scrutiny, no risk, no compassion or sympathy or anything close to eloquence. By the strident and aggressive tenor of the talk you couldn't tell if this BH entertained any doubt, then or ever, she was so careful not to cross herself, so careful to arrange her moral outrage along the lines of least resistance. In a sense the whole program was about BH rendering the round world flat and endorsing lopsidedness, halfness. This seemed a crude and retrogressive project since what really distinguishes us from apes is not the opposable thumb but the ability to hold in mind opposing ideas, a distinction we should probably try to preserve.

But these days you get the impression people think it's kind of recreant to waver, as if by feeling and expressing or worst of all admitting doubt and uncertainty you're being disloyal to a guiding idea. In the case of Mary Kay Letourneau it seemed to me that over the previous nine months what you had was the spectacle of this woman who'd been publicly knocked down, disgraced, humiliated, scorned, abandoned, who'd been imprisoned and made destitute, who'd lost everything, her family, her job, her house, her reputation, her freedom, her privacy, and even if I accepted the hardest line of the moral hardliners, even allowing for the possibility that this "adulterous" and "abusive" woman deserved what she got, that her crimes were staggering and odious and the probationary sentence just handed down by Judge Linda Lau was too lenient, that didn't stop me from feeling uncomfortable and real lonely as I listened to this brave and pharisaic Bonnie Hart, who from the safe defilade of her radio booth was basically bending over to pick up the first stone.

In a "situation" like this it's worth considering why only the authorities, the experts, the credentialed explainers remain articulate. Anyone alive today has at his or her disposal ages of mental experience to draw upon, and yet we seem to trust and accept only the most recent orthodoxies, the latest theories, the newest and freshest ideas in the marketplace. I applaud this reliance on the red-hot and the new when it comes to landing airplanes or doing appendectomies. Elsewhere, however, it seems we're just skimming the surface to locate the most recently revised version of ourselves, a tentative, experimental understanding. A long backward glance establishes pretty clearly what's endured over time and also exposes a lot of discredited stuff that was once taken quite seriously. I'm not just talking about the obvious crackpots and charlatans, nor do I mean the briefly credible phrenologists and lobotomists and such, but rather the discarded, the outmoded, the no-longer tenable, like, say, the ptolemaic astronomers and the reign of geocentrists that lasted a long two millennia. Even Marx and Freud, our last two great systematizers, show signs of wear and exhaustion after just a single century of application. Experts in every field hold holy models and systems, languages, understandings, that are themselves subject to challenge, revamping, innovation, further sectarian squabbles, and so the whole reeling thing bravely wobbles on, even under the administration of people whose intentions are of the highest order. They're dedicated. They keep up. Offices around this city are right now jammed with journals, trade publications, notes for papers and lectures, a whirlwind schedule of symposia stretching out over the upcoming calendar year, whatever, but it's not really possible (nor really desirable) to declare finality of understanding within a single discipline.

And so we improve one prejudice to rest awhile in another, we believe errors, we correct, reverse earlier decisions, advance again, struggle pitifully, and meantime as we revise and roll on Letourneau is caught in the amber of our understanding. This sense of understanding as fossil sample occurred throughout the story and after many readings of just about everything written on the Letourneau case I entered a near-mad state of chicken/egg confusion where habitual priority starts flipping around, and I couldn't tell anymore if people were trying to understand and describe Letourneau or invent a theoretical prototype. I started being unable to understand the words people were using, I couldn't make sense of Trust and Manipulation and Adultery and Power Base and Exploitation and Teacher, and other than this being ample evidence of why I'm not a judge or a lawyer or a doctor or a cop or for that matter anybody with any meaningful responsibility or position in this world and giving me a real sorrowful glimpse of why that's probably a very good thing, I also began to believe that of course Letourneau had to be sentenced, that sentencing her was a way of stabilizing the language. She upset accepted meaning, and I have no problem with Judge Lau's decision. That's not my concern here. What I wonder about is language, about what gets lost when laypeople concede the control of words to clinicians, scientists, lawyers, etc., which is, scilicet, the rich supple instrumentation of language that makes it an encounter with reality, that lets it reach into everything, into every little part of life, and how in this case a circle had formed and experts with fixed language were returning Letourneau to a fixed state, and doing so by excluding, again and again, notions that were not naturally a part of their descriptive vocabulary, like love.

Even though in the following quote I'm cutting a little bit against the grain of her intention, I think Lucy Berliner of Harborview Medical Center framed the problem succinctly when she said, "Even if (Letourneau) does genuinely have feelings for him, there is no context for a relationship like this to be normalized."

No context, where? In the language of sociology, law, psychology, victimology, penology, pedagogy? And what's "a relationship like this"? What's the omitted word? And why select the evasive, hesitant, nonspecific word "feelings"? And why the qualifier "even if"? And what's the difference between saying "even if she does *genuinely* have feelings for him" and saying "even if she has *genuine* feelings for him"? (Opting for the weak adverb instead of the adjectival form basically cripples Letourneau's action and in subtle syntactic ways indicates her feelings were never genuine or real in the object-noun world but only in her head, a shift in the direction of subjectivity which feeds right into the psyche-soc agenda, the fixing-up or at least identifying of errant bad-acting people with defective heads. It's all very neat and circular, and the system of Berliner's sentence is well-tuned.) But right now this is Einstein's world and both trains are moving so I want to go back briefly and look at the idea of the discarded. This is pretty common in the sciences, the abandoning of paradigms and the languages that go with them (see Thomas S. Kuhn, *The Structure of Scientific Revolutions*). In contrast, we don't discard the anguish of a father bent over his dead daughter (King Lear) or a man making a Faustian pact with the bitch goddess Success to win back the love of a woman (Gatsby) and so on. Further, we don't discard the language that creates this stuff either. In the case of King Lear the language that lets us see his magnificent ruin has outlasted Newtonian optics. Science deals with things, not human beings, and is speechless.

Fifty years ago Paul Tillich wrote, "It seems that the emphasis on the so-called 'empirical' method in theology has not grown out of actual theological demands but has been imposed on theology under the pressure of a 'methodological imperialism,' exercised by the pattern of natural sciences." Basically he says there's been a corruption of theology by the encroachment of scientific understanding into places where it doesn't belong. This "methodological monism," or the idea that a single system can describe everything, spreads out and in imperial fashion colonizes chemistry, theology, the study of literature and history, etc. But, he writes, "reality itself makes demands, and the method must follow; reality offers itself in different ways, and our cognitive intellect must receive it in different ways. An exclusive method applied to everything closes many ways of approach and impoverishes our vision of reality." You never want to forget that the encounter with life comes first; and an ascendent methodology, foreign to the subject in the first place, shouldn't stand in the way of that encounter.

"Our descriptions are better," Nietzsche wrote of older stages of knowledge and science, "but we do not explain any more than our predecessors."

To examine the description/explanation problem let's look quickly at a column by Terry McDermott (TMcD) that ran in *The Seattle Times* on Sunday, November 16, 1997. Prefatorily: I have nothing good to say about this column. It was smug, it was mingy, it was a skimpy 800 words (Anna Karenina, in contrast to Letourneau, was given 800 pages before Tolstoy pitched her under a train) that hinged on a kind fallacious reasoning that had by the day of sentencing become a staple of casual analysis, namely that if Letourneau had been a man and X a girl we'd have no qualms about sentencing her to "four years in the joint."

Here's the song sung in rounds:

—Karil Klingbeil (Director of Social Work, Harborview Medical Center): "I doubt that had there been a male perpetrator, it would have resulted in the same sentence."

—Nancy Grace (Court TV): "And let me guarantee you that if these roles were reversed and a male teacher had had sex with a 12- or 13-year-old student there would be no question that he'd be sent to jail."

—Shannon Peddycord (Bothell resident, in a letter to the *Times*): "Can you imagine had this been Joe-Stud Teacher and the victim a curvy 13-year-old girl?"

—And TMcD (in his column):

"Mary LeTourneau, 35, a schoolteacher, has an affair with a 13-year-old boy, a former student of hers.

"The affair produces a guilty plea to charges of second-degree child rape. It also produces a baby and, last week, a suspended sentence.

"Mark Blilie, 42, a schoolteacher, has an affair with a 15-year-old girl, a former student of his.

"The affair produces a conviction for third-degree child rape and child molestation and four years in the joint for Blilie.

"What's wrong with this?

"I mean, other than the fact that both these people did horrible things, that they abused children and the hopes and trust of entire communities.

"What's wrong, of course, is the similarity of the situations and the vastly different outcomes.

"How did this happen?

"The answers are . . ."

First off, "the joint"—I love that hard-boiled tough-guy lingo. When TMcD uses it the meaning is deceptive and suggests a real familiarity, not with prison or jails or the justice system, but with the genre of film noir and detective fiction, a filtrated and highly stylized knowledge of the underworld. Or maybe it was borrowed from the mouth of Frank Sinatra circa 1955. At any rate, as language the word just kind of hangs there, archaic and referential. "The joint"—never mind that it's antique slang, it's also about the most colorful and decorative word TMcD uses in the column and thus calls attention to itself, asking for examination. In the piece it functions rhetorically by setting up a crusty hardened term to contrast with the softness of Letourneau's heart and her weak and womanish insistence on love, *love* being a word presumably not used a whole lot in the mean dark weary bleak Bogey-haunted Sinatra-soundtracked inky black-and-white precincts TMcD inhabits down around Fairview Ave.—except maybe to describe a desperate broad or femme fatale or some other pathetic delusional female type. In the course of his column that softness of the heart, of her tendrilled hair, of a love that "mystifies everyone but her" is roundly dismissed, and TMcD's manly argot, the inner language of the knowing, is triumphant. Aided by this trope he concludes what everybody else concludes and does so by eliminating the mystifying element, love, from the equation.

"But when good people do bad things and do them on purpose, we are left without our normal, comforting rationalizations. It's very scary because in the end we are left to wonder: what about us?"

Thus ends the flow of rhetoric, on a note of pretend wonder. Tonally this piece took condescension to familiar heights for *The Seattle Times*. To begin, who exactly does that possessive include? It's my feeling TMcD's "our" refers, not to mine or yours, but to his and, by extension, the *Times'* "normal, comforting rationalizations" and that with this statement he's entered metajournalistic territory, sort of embedding a ghostly self-reflexive footnote to himself about the nature of the newspaper business and its questionable ability to cover anything that isn't "normal," etc. What's "scary" here is the paper's brief venture outside its objective stance and into the mysterious and confusing moral universe, a place it probably doesn't belong. Put differently the *Times,* with its protectorate sensibility, its wooden prose, and its stolid remove from the fray, is really just trying to tidy up the universe in the image of itself. I can't tell, but it kind of seems to me from many readings of the final paragraph that TMcD's blaming Letourneau for failing to clarify herself into a cliché à la Veronica Lake, that he's accusing her of being beyond understanding, of not fitting his story, of eluding his dated language, of monkeying with his sense of the normal, the comforting, the rationalized. Ergo we get "scary." Withal the entire column is written in the storybook language and syntax of a Junior Scholastic reader, providing a universe of "good people" and "bad people," a world where things are "very scary" or a fuzzy warmth is evoked by acknowledging that in situations like this "the answers are as simple as human history, and as complicated as the human heart."

A sentence like that sounds awfully resonant but you have to wonder if the writer in laying down the words had anything real in mind beyond the creation of sound effects. Read the sentence more than once and the vaguely axiomatic philosophical construction, the balanced but weary knowledge of the world's ways, the parallel repetition of *human*, the apposing of *heart* and *history*, might give you, as it did me, the sense of a sentence whose meaning probably mystifies everyone but the writer.

The easy interchangeability of the terms (if Letourneau were a man, X a girl) strikes me as a queer and cruel exercise in abstract thinking that depends on a mistake and a horrible forgetting. The mistake is to confuse what's merely similar with what's equal—"nothing is really equal" (Nietzsche)—and then pass it off as logic. On even the superficial level there seem to be plenty of differences between the two situations, but on the existential level there is nothing but difference. Letourneau and Mark Blilie are two different people, not data, not exempla, not variables awaiting quantity or value in a math equation. And this leads to the forgetting. What kind of damage is done to our ability to love or understand and thus fully judge one another when daily we're encouraged to forget people are people and view them instead as so much pasteboard, scenery, clutter, generalized instances (of murder, of rape, of embezzlement, etc.)? Here's a confounding particular: from what I've been able to gather, the boy the child the victim X is actually a couple inches taller than Letourneau. In terms of physical gifts alone he's a young man. But this was never brought up in the *Times/Post-Intelligencer* reportage, although it would, it seems to me, slightly alter or maybe completely redo a reader's picture of the child the boy the victim. Certainly it would affect your understanding.

There is in the press that will toward allegory, that tendency to find the model in every situation, to treat the swiftly passing moments of a vivid and specific life as illustrations in a large, stable, highly abstracted story. But what if the case of Letourneau does not apply to you and me in any parabolic sense? What if it's singular and freakish? What if it's exceptional, elusive? Where do we turn if we want to fully understand life in this anomalous form?

———

"The sympathetic heart is broken," D. H. Lawrence wrote. "We stink in each other's nostrils." Perhaps this harsh assessment of the modern soul is true, but perhaps what's also true, today, is we no longer even smell each other. One Florence Wolfe (affiliated with an outfit called Northwest Treatment Associates) prefaced a televised discussion of "the situation" by claiming she "had no sympathy" for Letourneau. This struck me as a bizarre kind of prophylaxis. She was basically holding her nose. You can hardly explain anything without explaining the explanation and thus risking a regressive free fall, but here goes. "The great secret of morals is love; or a going out of our own nature, and an identification," P. B. Shelley wrote. "A man must imagine intensely and comprehensively; he must put himself in the place of another and of many others . . . the great instrument of moral good is the imagination . . ." Just so I don't come across as a total poet-loving fruitcake (it's just that the interests of language were underrepresented in this case, that's why I keep bringing in these witnesses, these poets and novelists), Adam Smith—a free-market economist!—also helped make central the sympathetic identification imagination allows us to extend to others. And Keats refined the idea further in his famous letter on negative capability, describing a state in which "man is capable of being in uncertainties, Mysteries, doubts . . ."

(This is not to say that I think we'd be better off if these poets, these drunks, suicides, melancholiacs, queers, and ninnies were heads of state, only that they provide us the best record we have of the shifting sensitivities of language, the changes that in turn most carefully register movement in our evolving consciousness.)

At any rate by the eighteenth, nineteenth century, imagination is seen as a pretty important epistemological faculty and one of its key ingredients happens to be sympathy. This general idea hasn't entirely disappeared, despite various attacks, most of them non-philosophic-intellectual-academic and instead technological, economic, geographic—whatever, but still, it seems odd that an expert who presumably we've turned to for insight preannounces as a kind of caveat that sympathy is going to be removed from the equation of her understanding. Other experts did the same thing, e.g. Patrick Gogerty from Childhaven who was quoted postsentencing in the *Post-Intelligencer* as saying "this is pure and simple exploitation of a child" when quite clearly there was nothing pure or simple about the situation and the conditions (purity, simplicity) imposed on his point of view were just a framing device used to narrowly focus the idea of "exploitation" by excluding other, wider possibilities. This, *I* don't understand. "Imagination," Wordsworth said, "is amplitude of mind." But maybe sympathy's just a pain in the ass, maybe a sympathetic understanding would only muddy the works on television when all that's being asked for is a minute or two of high-cost clarity. Maybe a reasonable person understands you have to sacrifice certain things if you want your face on the small screen. And so in a devil's pact with the boob tube you unload your ballast of sympathy in order to deliver clarity, maintaining the *au fond* quality of your expertise, which is the providing of rock-solid and irrefutable and immobile answers. That is, you deliver ideas, insights, opinions, etc., as things. But why should I concede Florence Wolfe authority when it seems to me she's stated in advance that she plans to use only a limited perspective on the matter? She pulls out a pin and puts a prick in Wordsworth's amplitude of mind, deflating it just a little, and at that moment disqualifies herself, it seems to me, as someone to take seriously.

A couple in-court observations.

First, the two psyche-experts, Dr. Moore for the defense and Dr. Wheeler for the prosecution. What interested me most about their respective turns on the stand was the props they used and how those props differed and perhaps reflected their positions more succinctly than either doctor's windy recondite testimony. Moore fixed a big paper tablet to an easel and beginning significantly with a blank page used a red felt pen to draw a diagram that continued for several flowing pages. The paper was wrinkled and rough and the doctor's hurried handwriting was illegible. Her diagram forked and forked again with hasty hypomanic enthusiasm and was almost instantly an incomprehensible madly branching maze, but the interesting thing was to watch her make it up, like Harold with his Purple Crayon, as she moved forward, flipping to new pages, new ideas, new possibilities. You never knew what might happen next. Wheeler, by way of contrast, came to court with his chart already decided and drawn up, a one-page rectangular placard preprinted with blocky text and bulleted items. From where I sat in the cheap seats his chart looked like the last line in a doctor's eye examination and was also unreadable. In fact, I'm guessing no one in the courtroom could read either doctor's signs. It was kind of absurd. The easel angled away from both the bleacher full of journalists and the judge and was too far away for the rest of us to read and there was no jury who might need a visual aid to keep things straight, so what was the point? Moore's chaotic and bifurcating diagram captured and reflected her contentions about the bipolar state of Letourneau's mind and also created an image of liberty with its ever-forking and freely wandering path into the future; Wheeler's pre-arranged display offered a clear and orderly image of the future he was advocating for Letourneau, which was a clear sentence, a box, jail. While Moore's display moved through time, Wheeler's was static in time; hers evolved, his did not. Sitting there you kind of wondered to what extent each doctor's chosen method of image-creation reflected not an understanding of Letourneau but an insight into their (the doctors') personalities, thus also it raised a doubt about the solidity and objectivity of their science and their assessment of the case.

Second, I have to admit to large amounts of unprofessional rock-butt and boredom, which I was able to alleviate by occasionally shifting in my seat and closing my eyes and listening to the sounds of people's voices. But with my eyes closed I made a discovery. I heard the prosecuting attorney speak in two distinct voices. She used a sarcastic, dismissive voice while grilling Dr. Moore and another really irritating voice, hard to describe, but sort of storybook-sorrowful, the kind of voice you dip down into to read a tale's sad parts to a child, when she was giving her summation. Now I come from a pretty much jail-free family and none of us are lawyers and so my courtroom experience, before that morning, was nil. And attorneys I've seen in TV shows need to convince me primarily as actors and only secondarily as lawyers—the TV case, in other words, is decided on good or bad drama, not law—so nothing had prepared me for the bad acting, the transparent, awful acting, on the part of the real-life prosecutor, Lisa Johnson. Especially during the summation her voice tried to offer the aural image of concern, of gravity, of direness, but it was nowhere near the real thing itself. Her voice carried no genuine conviction and came off as sentimental, attempting to force on me, the listener, a feeling that was not there, that wasn't earned. And while I understand she's a lawyer, not an actor, still, that day, she played two different characters in court and then a third outside, using three very different voices. There was the Sarcastic and the Sentimental and lastly the Press Conference voice, and I only bring this up and think it's worth noting because in contrast Letourneau, in all the taped interviews I watched and listened to, in all the stories I read, never feigned emotion, never once took on, even for effect, a false character.

Third, Letourneau was given a chance to speak and did rise and say a few words and wanted to say a few more but the press interrupted and all at once started shooting photos of her. Cameras clicked like locusts, making an amplified mandibular chewing sound. It was an unbelievably ugly, swinish, and rude moment but so far as I know it's not been mentioned anywhere in the accounts of that day, a little omission about how Letourneau wanted to speak and was literally cut short and silenced by the media.

The law and the courts said Letourneau's crime was the rape of a child in the second degree. Shrinks for both the defense and the prosecution argued it was the sequela of a sickness, it was "hypomania" or a flaw in her "decision-making algorithm." Experts talked of abuse and rationalization and exploitation pure and simple. TMcD said it was just generically "scary." No one in or out of court bothered to bring in an ace authority on either love or language, so I'll do it myself, I'll swear in Gustave Flaubert, who wrote that "fullness of soul can sometimes overflow in utter vapidity of language, for none of us can ever express the exact measure of his needs or his thoughts or his sorrows; and human speech is like a cracked kettle on which we tap crude rhythms for bears to dance to, while we long to make music that will melt the stars." Anyway, you could see the day of the sentencing, as experts in psychology and sociology and law summed up and asserted their positions, how language was being leveraged, how each fragmented field with its highly specific problem-solving vernacular was in a way carting off pieces of Letourneau, and how in the end there was nothing left of the very thing she had probably hoped would unify her shattered life, this elevated, fanatical, rule-exempt, healing notion of love. The courtroom side of things lasted less than three hours. Afterwards there were cluster press conferences on the front lawn. Experts, specialists, lawyers, and whatnot kept insisting—this, that, etc.—but the whole before/after aspect of the sentencing was lost on me because, following the judgment, nobody had anything new to say.

Whaling

The whale's belly is simply a womb big enough for an adult. There you are, in the dark, cushioned space that exactly fits you, with yards of blubber between you and reality . . .
                                                —George Orwell

Four in the morning and I crawl out of the tent, thinking, what's my penis for, anyway, other than pissing? Actually as a man I've never been all that roosterly or priapic so what I'm likely thinking about is not my penis but late itchy procreant urges and babies. Or maybe deep down what I'm really considering isn't babies but the worthless legacy of my carcass in toto and the way the Makah once used whale for drains, combs, toys, tools, oil, etc., for all that artifactual stuff in their fine, fine museum, and how flattered I'd be if my bones, my hair, my eyeballs, my skull and hide, if all my remains, now and at the hour of my death and the day after, meant the world to someone. What high praise to have your sacrum worked and whittled into scrimshaw and bric-a-brac or to have your occipital carved into a comb and drawn down through some lovely woman's long brown hair! Or merely to be remembered, to have told three pretty good jokes or made a funny face or cooked up a batch of pancakes in some kind of special way or done anything at all of lasting anecdotal quality. But none of that's likely in my case, when I go. Unless the gravedigger whistles a hymn as he works probably no one'll even say a prayer.

I touch a stove-match to the mantle of my lantern and open the jet way up to full blast so its greenish light will beacon my way back to the tent and then I dance on tip-toes through the fog and over the cold packed sand toward the sea. I've got to piss but have decided I want to stand in the Pacific Ocean, about up to my knees. The canker of self-consciousness has been long in me, so like a lot of writers I not only do a thing, I see myself doing it too—it's almost like not being alone. That morning our hero skipped in his skivvies down to the shore of the sea . . . it was dark . . . the fog . . .

Storytelling!

In fact the fog's so dense and obliterating that this predawn offers a prospect as hopeless and unappealing as waking in heaven would after about the third day into eternity. And it is dark out but kind of white-dark like a chalkboard poorly erased. There's gooey sea-lettuce and other kinds of kelp underfoot and I can't really see. A wave washing around my ankles or perhaps a crease of white foam curling over in the sand will have to indicate a cautionary line where it's wise to stop or maybe not, maybe not, maybe walk on into the ocean, trust that the handful of people I haven't failed will remember me fondly, round things off right now and call it a life, make a biography out of this otherwise open aimless business.

Find closure!

One of Freud's disciples, Ferenczi I believe, developed what was known as the Thalassal Theory, in which a man, in coitus, is supposedly trying via vigorous humping to shake loose or snap off his penis and send it forth in a sort of ambassadorial role, northward into the woman's womb, thus returning anadromously to his natal home.

Science!

Back inland my tent's a bright illumined bubble such as good witches might live in. Next to the Constitution and Baseball and the Roadside Billboard (loneliness in space) and the All-night Diner (loneliness in time) I'd have to say the Coleman Lantern probably occupies fifth place on my list of great American contributions to civilization. No other lantern will do. The whisper and hiss and cranky dyspeptic sputter of a Coleman is as distinct and holy a music as the rev of a Harley. I like the celestial quality of the light, Venusian and green, the rounded simplicity of the mantle, the paint job, of course, and the way one sounds when swung by the bail. I've hauled the extra pounds of a Coleman up into the mountains when it might have been more commonsensical to sit in the dark or scratch in my journal by candlelight or bag words altogether and mindlessly stare at the stars. And while I enjoy solitude I like as much the convivial feeling of encampment in crowded parks where families chatter and rehash fables and legends of the comical father while Coleman lanterns light up and start the shadows of all the lovely mothers jitterbugging against the walls of trailers as they stow away the hot dog buns.

This time out I'm alone, it's dark, but I haven't worried about the boogeyman in years; too often, though, I've brought a case of troubled love out to this uncaring coast. Dating way back, I can recall a catalog of poignancies. What's remained constant over the years is a sense that when you're alone you're prey, or feel at least it's potentially your fate to be stalked and eaten. Of course the benefits of being on your own include a certain vital spunk and a dexterity that comes to life when you're unencumbered, a spring in the step that keeps you ahead of the pack. Player and pep rally both, you cheer yourself on. Go! Yet everywhere beyond yourself is a bigness, a forest, a vault of stars, the surface of the sea, or the city at midday, ready to give you a drubbing. You vs. just about everything else. Alone, you're vastly outnumbered; but in the company of another, by some weird miracle of human math, the odds seem wonderfully improved in your favor.

Save the whales!

I have to confess I came out to this last, far corner of the country hoping to eat some whale. I came with the idea of getting a mathematically insignificant chunk of meat off a gray whale that washed ashore several years ago and was flensed on the beach and supposedly doled out by the Makah to every member of the tribe. It was like a roadkill whale, half of it necrosed and putrid and bound for the Neah Bay dump, half of it salvaged and stowed in freezers. This particular stranded whale maybe weighed 20 tons or 40,000 pounds (while the estimated number of extant grays currently stands at 23,000 total or by my loose estimates a whopping 1,702,000,000 pounds) and what I wanted was hardly more than a pork chop's worth of whale, maybe a pound, so that I might sample a tiny piece of the controversial behemoth myself. I just wanted to eat some. The Catholic in me thought eating a little leviathan—which I prayed would not in any way remind me of chicken, and suspected would taste like a petroleum product, say a bike tire or Vaseline—might bring me sacramental or at least alimentary insight. Foolishly I thought I'd just breeze into Neah Bay, pick up some whale, and flame broil it for breakfast. I wasn't sure if whale was traditionally a breakfast food but I'm not a Makah nor a student of indigenous peoples or aboriginal lifestyles and I'm generally not inclined to go native so anthropologic fidelity wasn't a big concern of mine. All I knew was I hoped to skewer and roast a piece of gray whale and feed the first honorary tidbit off this sort of cetacean shish kebab to my dog, experimentally, after which I thought I might even try it myself.

I packed in some stomach remedies in case I got lucky.

The supposed cuddly quality of cetaceans I just don't get. Between barnacles and sea lice the few whales I've seen up close were hideously, hoarily disfigured or at least blemished and tactilely repellent the way certain so-called—not by me—pizza-faced teenagers are. I've seen stray grays in the Sound, come to shore to scratch their backs in Saratoga Passage, and they've all had a mottled gray pocked aspect, like poured cement. Their souls may be infinitely sweet and poetic, possessed of an earnestness and bonhomie I can only envy, but their bodies, in terms of color and surface texture, resemble bridge abutments. Not that these monsters shouldn't show a little wear and tear after making a yearly migration of 14,000 miles round-trip so that, by the time the average gray is twenty, it's traveled 280,000 miles, or swum, basically, to the moon—which is truly awesome. It probably also explains that corroded crudded-up look. Gray whales get used roughly, making their migratory haul through Siberia, the Gulf of

Alaska, etc., on their way south to the warm buoyant waters and calving grounds of Baja California. That's no frolic. That's a hell of a lot of use for any kind of carcass.

An encounter with a gray whale is bizarre and if your first sighting happens unticketed and outside the enervated sanction of a tour it'll seem contextually spooky and saurian. Gray whales don't look especially dirigible. You'd hate to have to park one. They have a lumpy crudeness of design, a banged-up body and a crimped ugly mouth and a dented snout, a color that seems to come from a supply of government surplus paint, and all-around they have an unrefined and ancient and also untrustworthy aspect; they look like a mock-up of the kind of practice mammals God was making in the early days before he hit his artistic stride and started turning out wolves and apes and chipmunks; and they've got that useless megaton bigness, a gigantism that's pretty dramatic in a circus-freak way or like other types of colossi or prodigies, the sheer extravagant enormity of which inspire sublime fascination or wonder or fear but don't register much at the refined and fragile end of the emotional spectrum that includes the various colors of love or tender or chummy feelings of any sort. I myself can't square forty tons of whale flesh or even the word *blubber* with what I know about sweetness and intimacy; they're not ducklings or kittens or puppies or little lambs or fawns or piglets. In fact their very bulk seems inimical to closeness, to holding and embracing, but maybe, baby-freak that I've lately become, I can now only conceive of love in liftable forms, as something you put your arms around.

My numinous boyhood belief was that whales rose to the surface because they were lonely, tired of the depths. Their ancient bulk seemed to body forth exactly what it meant to be solitary, but breaching and spouting a sigh of relief through the blowhole in their head they lost some of their august self-sufficiency and were always depicted in familial groups, rather frolicsome and sweet, desirous of good company, of community. Obviously I was equating depth with darkness and darkness with cold and cold with silence and all of the above with a nearly insane state of isolation—okay, with my father—whereas things on the sunny maternal surface of *la mer* seemed to enjoy the sort of warm lapping buoyancy necessary for cultivating friendship and love. The story of Jonah reinforced this spatial arrangement, as did *Moby Dick* later, where Pip sinks a fathom too far into the sea's immensity and comes up mad and/or mantic. But things have changed. Nowadays it's just as likely the surface of life is what puzzles Pip and finally sends him around the bend, and today's cabin boy must go alone into the quiet depths to escape and find peace and recover for himself a measure of sanity. It's civilization that's raw and wild and full of scary monsters and grotesques and deformities crowding every bus and park bench and court of law whereas we now believe our wilderness exhibits the high sweet harmony we hope for from life as well as offering the refuge and sanative balm we desire when our energies flag and the botch of civilization gets us down.

Paul Watson's floating around somewhere out there in the very same fog as me, Captain Paul Watson of the Sea Shepherd Conservation Society. He seems to have commandeered the environmentalist argument—and there's a creepy uncritical parroted quality to what every-body else in the pro-whale (or is it anti-Indian) camp is saying—and his main, openly stated fear (as opposed to his real agenda, of which, more later) seems to be the precedent the Makah hunt will set for other whaling nations. But if the problem really is the recrudescence of commercial whaling and wide-scale industrial slaughter, then the Japanese ought to be taken to task for their rapine, or the Norwegians, or whoever, but it's a pretty specious argument that can make the corruptions and failures of these people somehow the direct fault of the Makahs. It's a sophistic argument, in fact, but Paul Watson's not much of a logician; he's mostly a misanthrope and a sentimentalist (how often those things go together!), sweet on whales and sick about what he calls "base-virtued" humans, and his rock-ribbed stance re: the hunt is all about the lone whale, soulful and solitary, perhaps a poet, singing songs, echolocating down the coast, intelligent, gentle, sentient, loving, unfairly ambuscaded (by heathens!) while going about its business—pretty much the otherworldly and animistic whale of my boyhood.

There's not now nor was there probably ever a shortage of love for Indians in the noble and rhetorical abstract but even more abundant and pressing has been a heap-big annoyance at the nuisance created by Injuns that are actually alive and walking around and scratching their bellies and grumbling about what's for dinner or listening to the radio or reading books or arguing over the rules of Monopoly and especially those that are rather clamorous (uppity) about their needs. It all gets so queer and drifty and hard to track these days. Eco-Elements on First Ave. downtown has been instrumental in gathering signatures for a petition against the Makah, and it's one of those New Age emporiums with a syncretic, boutiquey approach to spirituality, a sort of travel agency specializing in tourism for the soul, emphasizing past lives, future lives, every kind of life but the really incompliant and unruly present, where Tarot, Runes, Goddess-stuff, Astrology, Native American Spiritual Resources, healing soaps and oils and aromas, candles that calm you down and bells that strike a special, particularly resonant and congenial note—where all this totally creeps out the stodgy defunct Pauline Catholic in me, and yet—yet!—this reaching out to the arcane holy world, this Luddism of the soul, however fey and preposterous and apostatic and pagan it might seem in my eyes—you'd think this grab bag of atavistic practices would put the New Ageists in deep and direct sympathy with the Makah.

But it doesn't. And not so weirdly, a lot of the attacks on the Makah seem to gut and hollow out the "Indian" and take that rhetorical material and use it as stuffing which in turn is packed into whales. The clichés about Indians transfer easily into clichés about whales, similar in substance and similarly hackneyed, yet housed in different vessels. The noble savage qua noble mammal. This can't be flattering to the Makah while I imagine metaphor in general is probably a matter of oceanic indifference to even the most poetic gray whale. And the rhetorical violence—the stealing of language, the silencing—shouldn't surprise anyone even remotely versant with white/Indian history. Captain Watson likes to footnote his superior credentials as an Indian enthusiast from way back—Wounded Knee!—and yet somehow without tearing his brain in half he's able to plunge ahead with low, vicious, even paranoid attacks on the Makah as people. A small measured dose of irony should prevent this kind of mental sloppiness, but doesn't, probably because people in the environmental movement, like holy folks everywhere, don't make real keen ironists. I can pretty well guess that these sort of merit-badge Indians aren't entirely or enthusiastically embraced by your average enrolled tribal member, especially as they listen to Watson float pseudo-arguments that asperse the character of the Makah and accuse them of being liars, frauds, cheats, racketeers, colluders, and, of all things, fake Indians.

Abstract love is the nosy neighbor of abstract hate; they see right into each other's windows and they always agree on everything. And neither one of them really tests disinterestedness, the ability to make tragic choices between things of equal worthiness and legitimacy—which to my mind explains why so much writing and discussion about whales tends toward melodrama, where right and wrong are always clear, where only one of the terms is justified. "The opposition are not nice guys," Captain Watson has written. Nice? That seems a simpy word for a big old jackpot of a problem, a lazy and sinister trope suggesting that to oppose (Paul Watson) is to lack niceness, by definition. "I have no time for the arguments of tradition," Watson, the honorary Indian, has written. And further: "I have no wish to understand them. I have no wish to argue the pros and cons of whaling." He says, "The tradition of whalekind is of far more value to me." And this tradition comprises what? "They (the whales) grace the azure blue with a majestic intelligence wedded to an amazing tactile grace. A profound, elusive, ephemeral sentience, they deify the abysmal depths with their regal presence." If you can love abstractly, you're only a bad day away from hating abstractly. Somehow mere difference has been torqued up and given a moral dimension; by way of solution we know the next step—wearying to think of as this century wanes away—is to call for the annihilation of all distinctions.

The real high-ass muck-a-mucks of the pro-whale debate like to think they cut somewhat quixotic figures, noble, paladin, but the environmental movement in the matter of the whale hunt hasn't represented the best thinking by the best people; it's been a disaffecting display, at least for me. Where are the eloquent American saints, where is Thoreau, where Emerson, Muir, Marshall, Leopold, Olson, Abbey? Even David Brower for god's sake! It's too bad Watson's so blinkered because the man knows cetaceans, as a student of the species and a hands-on advocate, better than anyone. He sees the situation, globally. His knowledge of whales is compendious and compassionate, but in public, dealing with people, he comes off as a bullying prig—his manners on *Town Meeting* were particularly appalling. With broader vision—a vision that extends to people even an ounce of the generosity he lavishes on whales—he might really help sort this mess out. He might even be able to broker a deal. He could wrangle concessions. But Watson seems paranoid whenever he's writing about whales; in one astonishing sort of Christic psychomachy (*Sea Shepherd Log*, spring 1997) he relates the tale of his conversion, his Damascus experience, his baptism in whale blood, and puts himself across as a persecuted man, a prophet and savior. This messianic aspect of the movement, its higher, holier purity, is hard to stomach. It's theocratic and imperial and arrogant and because of it Watson comes across as just another flawed man and broken reformer hiding his human failings behind another lofty and immaculate and inviolate cause.

The acronymic groups—PAWS, AFA, SSCS, PETA, etc.—who've organized opposition to the Makah hunt don't go for killing sea mammals under any circumstances. That's really their stance, and, boiled long enough, the irreducible core of their case. This intractability has lent a sullen and futile feel to the debate, a mudslinging, lie-swapping, smug, accusational tone that, rather than clearing the air, actually just fouls and debases anybody and everybody who joins in. These people have made up their minds; there's never been any room to maneuver. They're into whales, and not real fond of humans. In fact they seem to favor any of God's creatures over the malignant cancer of humanity. Their misanthropy takes the metaphoric exuberances of the late odd brilliant crank Edward Abbey literally, which is always scary. I mean from Christ to Nietzsche we know it's one thing when the rich voice of a solitary radical shouts out and it's another thing when the echo of the ochlocratic chorus comes roaring back in agreement. Suddenly a certain kind of valence is gone. Abbey was a philosopher, wit, pisser, and prose stylist, and one of the first qualities sacrificed by his adherents is the anarchic soul of a man who claimed the Peace Corps was a "piece of insolence," "an act of cultural arrogance." The kind of man who could litter and make the act seem deductive, radical, and exemplary. The kind of man who strongly advocated population control and yet fathered four children himself—but by five wives, he argued, which was, when you did the math, only .8 children per woman, well below the national average. But when the lesser souls pick up the program, they smooth out the saving contradictions, flatten the subtleties, excise the humor, empurple the prose, hoist the flag, and recite the pledge, and then march forth like fanatics and disciples and crusaders everywhere, ready for jihad and genocide.

Watson's been assigned the task of interpreting the psychograms sent to him by whales and apparently he's heard from the whales that they'd rather not be harpooned. His stated claim is he'd like to return whales to some state pre-everything—Eden, the womb—while the Makah in an obvious clash would in some measure like to return themselves to a pre-contact world, before Captain Vancouver, before Puget, Rainier, etc., and certainly before Captain Paul Watson showed up on the scene.

Myself, I really doubt the efficacy of the Makah project because generally I'm skeptical about movements to restore culture. Whether the project's conducted by Hitler or Mussolini, Yukio Mishima or Ronald Reagan, or fundamentalists in Iran, Lybia, or Idaho, or by Wovoca and the Ghost Dancers, or by modern communicants who raise their heads heavenward to receive the body and blood, I just don't think the hoped-for resurrection or the dream of a return to glory is viable. Randall Jarrell once wrote that even in the Golden Age people were always griping about how everything looked yellow; all our hopes elude us. Just as shadows fall across lives, history falls across cultures. Things unravel never to reknit again and contact quite likely brings with it the entropic doom Levi-Strauss talks about in *Tristes Tropiques*. Our complex intermingling kills. We wake out of our dreams and wonder where the blood on our hands came from. Knowledge happens just about as often as shit while innocence is probably returned to by taking yet another bite of the apple, not by pretending there never was a fall in the first place.

But my despairs are Western despairs and I really don't know a thing about the restorative capacity of the Makah soul.

Regardless, right or wrong, it's not up to me to judge the eventual cultural outcome for the Makah of killing a whale off the coast, and not because I'm indifferent to the fate of the environment, or because I agree or disagree with what the sloganeers for either side have to say about whales, but because the Makah are an independent people who ought to be able, for once, to fail on their own, without the encouragement of whitefolk. Or, vice versa, sort of, they ought to be allowed the chance to succeed without a boost from the BIA, HUD, IHS, Dept. of Interior, missionaries, social workers, tourists, etc., on terms they've developed by and for themselves. They might like for once to be free of the entangled bureaucracy of being Indian. Or they might like to paint their asses green and play hacky sack by moonlight. I don't know. I can't say. The intestine affairs of the Makah don't really interest me, although I'm certain within the community there are factions, pro and con and even indifferent, but probably what's not needed now is a lot of high-minded refereeing from the outside. They have a treaty, and really the hunting of this whale is about our honor. We need to think about ourselves.

Killing a whale the Makah way is a highly unique, specialized undertaking, and I can't imagine anyone doing it for kicks or as a show of bravado or even as an incautious stab at reviving culture. There are other ways to go about getting your daily bread, most of them drier and warmer.

At the Makah Museum there are a couple bow and arrow sets but they're really pathetic looking and I thought, seeing those flimsy toys, man, it's a pretty good bet these Makah probably didn't eat a whole lot of bear meat. The arrows were hardly longer or stouter than hot dog sticks; the bows didn't seem flexible or tensile enough to generate enough velocity to puncture hide let alone find the heart of a bull elk from forty feet. But then you walked around and saw the whale and seal harpoons and the massive halibut hooks and the fishnet ingeniously fabricated from nettles—nettles!—and you realized that here was the sphere where these people really kicked ass.

Even in the long gone Ozette olden days, five centuries ago, they had little baby harpoons for kids to play with, complete with mini-fingerholds, a kind of bridge or granny stick crotched for launching harpoons, so these little Makah boys would get the exact right feel of the weapon and begin to perfect their stroke from the moment they reared back and stuck their very first—I don't know—tree stump. What little Willie Mays's developed their form and a sense of the world's exact rightness playing with these sticks on the sandlot beaches of what's now the Makah Nation? And the big-league harpoons their daddies used—what fantastic inventiveness it must have taken to figure out the logistical details of that first hunt, what holy-making number of Makah bones are buried and scattered beneath the sea around Cape Flattery, what lives were lost, what women cried, what children wondered, what brothers went silent, while these men worked out the kinks in their whale-killing prowess. Some amazing man, some Moses of the Makah, had to have had a vision powerful enough to lure and lead the others on. That magical moment alone should be saved from extinction. Think on it—you take the biggest body of water in the world, and it's the edge of winter, it's maybe lonely and horrifying and you're melancholic in some affective disordered way and all around you there's an extra-heavy-duty cobalt rain battering down, and there at your feet on the beach you've got a pile of old bones and a couple tree branches and somehow, looking at them, and looking out to sea, somebody comes up with the idea of sticking a thirty-ton whale? It stuns the mind, it blasts and levels the imagination.

Up to my knees in nature, I get mighty cold, naturally. I shiver in paroxysmal fits and feel what's possibly the onset of hypothermic derangement, and so head back to the tent, dry off, do ten jumping jacks, then ten more, pull on a pair of clammy jeans and a fleece jacket and a goofy crushed duckcloth cap I favor in the fall, and start a fire. Twigs and bark and moss and a few credit card receipts to kindle the flame, larger sticks of driftwood propped tepee-style to keep it going. As I work and warm myself the sky lightens from one shade of unhopeful gray to another. I collected and chopped wood half the night, hoping to exhaust myself and hold bad thoughts at bay. It didn't work. Poise and stability are not about never moving but rather about nimbly keeping step with the world as it pitches and rolls below your feet—one of several Hallmark-isms I try to live by.

When I go to feed the dog I find I've forgotten to bring her bowl; I pull off my cap and fill that with kibble. The waxed cotton holds water nearly as well as it repels it and she laps up a cool hatful after eating. I smack the hat against my thigh and set it back on my head. For entertainment and edification I've got *The Audubon Book of Weather* and Pascal's *Pensées*, but right now I'm not in the mood to sit in the fog and read about fog nor do I, feeling skeptical and doubt-ridden, much care to read what the brilliant transit planner has to say about skepticism and doubt. My mood? Fuck the whales! This too is nature—all of it, and maybe when I get back to Seattle I'll place a personal in the *Weekly*, truthfully saying, like most do, that I'm into nature, the woods and long walks, red wine and fires and poetry, philosophizing and fucking, the dawn light and the starry night, and all the other inadequate and hugely depressing analogues for unique and heightened sensitivity.

The real tragedy in this state isn't the healthy run of migratory whales that hugs the coast in October/November but the passing of the salmon, the magnitude of which is equivalent in scale to the disappearance of sixty million buffalo from the plains in one short murderous span of the nineteenth century. Fewer and fewer people in the region have any memory of real, living salmon and seem satisfied with the bullshit touristy display of tossed fish at the market and so nothing will ever actually be done and those

Coho and Kings—Kings! Tyees!—are gone and gone, it's horrible to say, with a whimper. No single salmon is big enough to be a cause célèbre on its own whereas one whale the size of a Winnebago is, and so people notice. And, noticing, they get all drippy about whales, remotely enlivened and stirred to abstract opinion, when, in fact, the loss of salmon should rouse them to enormous, cetacean-sized outrage, and doesn't, since who cares where it comes from—salmon raised on farms! in frog ponds!— as long as filets and steaks of it are still served on plates around the city? Nary a salmon fighting to spawn in your local stream but down the street there's plenty cooling on beds of ice behind the local grocer's display case.

I had no luck getting any whale. I asked. I did. I made phone calls and inquired at the museum and stopped strangers on the street and said to my waitress at the diner, you don't have any whale, do you? I even checked the freezer section of the grocery store. Along the way many many Indians—men, women, and children, the old and the young, workers and loafers, thin, fat, tall and short, braided and shaved—laughed right in my face. They weren't unduly snickering or snide about it; generally the laughter was big, hearty, frank, and guffawish. They seemed to find in my question a new comical low point, even after months of talking to journalists.

No whale—so the meager larder I laid in for this trip includes a supply of Wellbutrin, Mylanta, ground coffee, a gallon of fresh water, a package of Hostess cupcakes, kibble for my dog Kala, and a fresh filet of salmon off a small resident silver I caught in the Sound the day before.

Communion

we worship
the salmon

because we
eat salmon

—Sherman Alexie

I prop open the hood of my truck, pull out the dipstick, burn the excess oil off in the fire, and skewer my salmon by interlacing four or five clumsy sutures through the skin. (Better prepared, I would've baked a few potatoes on the engine manifold. A woman in Montana told me I should always keep a can of black pepper in my tool kit, because in a pinch it'll plug a radiator leak. When I asked her if there were any other spices I ought to store in the car, she said an onion in your glove box isn't a bad idea for your DUI situations. Had I heeded her advice my truck would've been pretty much as fully equipped as my kitchen.) Anyway, I get my unadorned filet sizzling over the fire and the skin instantly starts dripping gobbets of crackling fat on the coals. I set some coffee on my stove and crank the flame. I lean back against a log and look at my watch, angling the face into the firelight. It's a quarter to five.

The men in my family have undone themselves in some kind of grand westering impulse gone awry. We ran out of land and then went one step further, west of west. We've shot ourselves and jumped from bridges and lost our minds and aborted some of our babies and orphaned others and now reproducing and carrying on the family name is down to me, and the truth is soul-wise I'm likely a bigger monster than either of my broken brothers or my father. As the extant capable male in my family I either perpetuate our name or wipe it off the earth forever. The hints about what I should do haven't been so awfully subtle that even a mental clodhopper like myself can't catch the drift. Nature in me has come up empty, and so be it. I figure it took thousands of years to make Irish and Italians of my grandparents; America undid that in a scant generation. We've come to nothing—so soon? Shine On, Perishing Republic! I'm not sure I want to be the dead end of it all but then again how would I really feel with my seed trailing after me, wanting things? The mythopoeia of my family now seems to say if we persist in any patronymic way that's history and destiny and if we die off then in some loop-the-loop of logic that turns out to be history and destiny as well, ha ha.

It's always been a fond Western dream, after all the blood and pavement and franchising, to undo the whole sorry business and begin again.

The first best seller in America was an epic poem by Michael Wigglesworth called "The Day of Doom." There's a beginning.

What's left to say?

I wish I had some children that were around going *Daddy Daddy* so I could provide a wise impartial answer or at least pour a glass of milk for them. Who needs Pascal— "When I consider the short duration of my life, swallowed up in the eternity before and after, the little space which I fill, and even can see, engulfed in the infinite immensity of spaces of which I am ignorant, and which know me not, I am frightened, and am astonished at being here rather than there; for there is no reason why here rather than there, why now rather than then."—since even without a philosophical assist my uselessness appalls me.

The fog's gone away like a ghost. I turn off my lantern. I pick my salmon off the dipstick and eat it with my fingers and watch to the south as a great confetti-ish flight of seagulls spins through the air. Behind me a sand-hill crane with an ungainly pterodactyl *whomp* lifts above the estuary of a river whose name I don't know; once aloft on its six-foot wings the crane soars in a circle with unlabored grace, landing back in the alluvial mud exactly where it began.

Where am I, in what land, in whose time?

Right this moment in the matter of Here vs. There I guess I'd rather be in some warm kitchen with little pieces of dirty chicken on the linoleum and last night's macaroni noodles underfoot and a pile of unwashed bobbies in the sink. And just exactly where are all the fine, tender, decent, steady, productive, forthright family-men in the world right now, men toward whom, in infrequent but fairly rhythmic, practically menstrual fits of waking horror, I feel jealous? Not on this beach, that's for sure. I guess my true Here will always be an Elsewhere. And so I've arrived in this strange place and it's okay for now, it's rich, it's really queer, it's made of the morning a kind of phantasmagoria, the stuff of dreams and fevers, and what was I really thinking anyway, that my phantom children, needing wisdom and milk, were supposed to be out here with me, pissing in the ocean too?

Modular Homes

Right inside the door of my first Fleetwood Home I was greeted by the evocative odor of American Newness, that smell everyone knows but cannot name. It was like breaking the seal on a box and getting a whiff of—of what?—of exactly what you always wanted. I know I got doped up on the smell and instantly forgot the facts of my life for the fantasy it might become. The walls in the homes I toured had the texture of those egg-shaped confections of sugar that house dioramic Easter scenes of bunnies and baby chickens. The walls didn't look entirely dry, as though you might sink your finger in for a lick of buttercream frosting. They were immaculate and white and somehow against this backdrop even normal objects seemed like miniatures, not quite real and thus easily manageable. All the rooms were furnished by a hired decorator but felt empty. What they were missing was you and yet it was haunting to confront a face in a mirror. Suddenly you were there, arrived and occupying a place in this world premised on choice, where everything exists as potential, where the deep pile carpet on the floor is only a polite suggestion and might, in a moment's wish, become Adobe, Cameo Blush, Cabernet, Cinnabar, Periwinkle, or Nappa (sic) Valley. The Formica on the counter could be traded for squares of blue tile. The fridge will find food, the quiet will find voices, the beds will bring rest and love and renewal.

To make a manufactured home first you build a chassis with axles. After you've put the chassis in place you glue and staple the flooring to it with extra-big boards that cut down on the number of seams and hence reduce the likelihood of leakage. As it's being built the house floats like a river barge on a bed of compressed air. A couple men lean into it with their shoulders and shove it from one station to the next as if it were nothing. Exterior walls go up, interior walls, men plumb the thing, run wires, install fixtures, they add windows, hang doors, a roof is lowered in place by an Erector-Set crane, appliances, cabinets, fans, and carpets are readied. Out of this wizardly and truly awesome Oz the house is wheeled into the daylight and trucked away to whatever Kansas your heart desires.

I made a couple trips to the factory and a dirt lot nearby where Fleetwood showcases their finished product, and lastly I started looking for places where I could find people living in the houses for real. Several detours off Interstate 5 showed me just how rapidly a community seeded with modular housing can grow. Everything's so brand-new there isn't even any sound in the air. In one such neighborhood off Gun Club Road in Woodland, Washington, I parked my truck and tried to talk to some kids coming home from school but they were right on it with the snappy, drilled response.

"Are you a stranger?" one little girl wanted to know.

"What's a stranger?"

"Somebody who kills you or rapes you," she said.

I'm not that kind of stranger, but it might have been here, in this neighborhood, in this place where the children know what to say, that a note of sorrow first entered the world of hope I'd been entertaining during my initial home tour.

Your typical manufactured home makes its way in the world because it bears a studied resemblance to a regular house. Its visual ambition is mimetic and realistic the same way a painting of a cow agreeably satisfies verisimilitude if it's got four legs, a tail, and a head. You could build these homes attractively but the aesthetic would need to be stripped and lean and frank, with materials that openly declare themselves and hide nothing. Fleetwood, by contrast, makes a sincere imitation of the real thing, a house that aspires to popularity and recognition like a girl who comes to the prom with a face on loan from a magazine. It's that inserted layer of sincerity that rings false. It's evilly un-American to say aloud, but real divisions exist between people, and the houses themselves try hard, desperately hard, to obscure those differences. They're socially insecure yet hopeful. They want acceptance and to get it they try really hard to please everyone.

The woman who gave me my factory tour was so sweet, so kind, so eager to encourage my optimistic assessment of Fleetwood's product, the echo of everything she said now rattles around in my head because I knew before I entered the building I'd betray her trust and hope. She told me she herself lived in a Fleetwood triple-wide and was absolutely happy. Like everyone connected with Fleetwood she was defensive against unspoken snottiness, and given my inability to rise above it I can see why. "I hope you say something nice," nice people kept saying to me in person and on the phone. Salespeople and secretaries alike insisted that a Fleetwood Home was every bit the structural and social equal of what's known in the trade as a stick-built house. Their zeal was evangelistic, it was memorized and rehearsed and recited like a prayer, it was felt and sincere and thus a notch shy of being spontaneously true. What people were telling me was no more a syncretic hodge-podge than the Pledge of Allegiance, but if you don't live entirely within it, if you're not un-self-consciously at home in the words and you hesitate even a little, it all starts to sound like cant.

In the face of so much generous and heartfelt uplift I cut short the factory tour, asking no questions. This woman and all these people, they are the good people, whereas I was just walking around in the factory faking my enthusiasm and hiding a creepy low-grade horror. Normally I don't like my meaning ready-made, but by the time I headed out to my truck I was in total despair about not being with the program.

I drove up along the Lewis River for a change of scene and to think and to see if anybody was catching fish from an early fall run of chinook. "A good attitude is a treasure," said the sign outside the Woodland Middle School, on my way upriver. Five miles back in the canyon the banks were crowded with fishermen working fairly dull obvious water, where the highly evolved homing instinct of the salmon hits the blunt obstruction of a dam and the fish pool up in mass confusion. At the hatchery there was the usual display of agitprop about salmon recovery and an article about the building of the first dam and how it might just possibly disrupt and ruin the runs. It did, of course, and now the Lewis is only the ghost of itself, flowing emptily into the Columbia. The article was written in 1930 and seventy years later the river no longer seriously produces salmon but continues to spin the turbines that supply power to the recessed lights in the kitchens of modular homes up and down I-5. An abiding American assumption, mentally apocalyptic, says that somehow the wrongs in history stem from our ignorance; once we're enlightened, we'll be free of the past and history itself will stop and we'll come to rest in a return to Eden. Now the state of Washington raises fish in rearing ponds and releases smolts into the river, hoping their intricate salmonoid nerves won't give out in complete bafflement and, after four years at sea, they'll find their way back upriver to the cul-de-sac of their birth. These ponds remind me somehow of Gun Club Road, of modular homes, and all our paradisal mythologies of return.

It wasn't my original plan but I checked into a motel for the night because it bugged me that I couldn't find anything nice to say about modular homes. I ate dinner at a Mexican restaurant across the street. It was karaoke night in a lounge the hostess referred to as "the cantina." The décor was modular Mexican, a sort of mañana peon style that lightly revamped clichés about lazy Mexicans. Two guys at my table told me they were hiding from their wives, they'd kind of karaoked a lie about working on their cars and instead had come to the cantina for a couple quick rum and cokes. Another guy's girlfriend was out of town and he kept asking me what I thought of the waitress's ass. He was embarrassing me and I felt square and stupid and unable to say what, as a man, I know I'm supposed to say, and so, nervously changing the subject, I asked him about the fishing on the Lewis. He said, "Look, we took the land from the Indians, like what? I don't know. Five hundred years ago? Was it five hundred years? Big deal. I'm all for paying them back, but after a generation, or two, they should get in society like everyone else." Later I shared a table with a woman whose home business was writing personal poetry "for your weddings and funerals." She often writes letters for friends who need special thoughts expressed and many people have told her she should write a novel. Her husband recently convinced her to leave Portland and move to Woodland and then he left her for the woman next door and moved back to Portland. Divorce and treachery and betrayal were in the air but so was desire and the people who came forward to sing surprised me by their earnestness. I'd have thought this kind of thing a joke, snide and ironic, but they sang their hearts out. The favored narrative of the songs people selected turned on love and heartbreak and while the music and the words were not the singer's own, the voice and the feeling were. Emotion was evident by the way people gripped the microphone and bowed their heads as they waited eight bars for the chorus to come around and when it did they lifted their heads again and sang the words and moved toward the crowd compelled by an inner urgency.

My last day I still didn't feel like going home. I lingered, pointlessly. Overnight a banner had been strung across

Woodland's main drag announcing the coming of "Make a Difference Day." I stopped a couple places to look through a few more completed houses. All along I'd been intrigued by the lack of language inside these model homes. There were no words, spoken or written, and even the few decorative books seemed mute on the shelves—not words, but things. Language in the modular industry belongs largely to the manufacturing end of the business, and there, in technical brochures and spec sheets, it's thick and arcane, made up of portmanteaus and other odd hybrids that are practically Linnaean in their specificity. You get Congoleum and Hardipanel Siding and Nicrome Elements. At the factory all that language is assembled and given narrative development in the tightly plotted path the house takes as it progresses from chassis to truck. But once inside the finished home it ends, there's a kind of white hush, a held breath, and all narrative, defined simply as a sequence of events in time, is gone. The paradisal urge toward silence and timelessness takes over so that when the door opens and you cross the threshold you feel you've stepped out of life itself.

In house #19 I find an icy aspect to the arrangement of family artifacts and like Keats before the Grecian Urn I can't quite puzzle out the story. Photos have been framed and set out on tables and shelves but the pictures are of those same corny people who haven't aged a bit since they came with your first cheap wallet. Who are these blonde

women with unfading smiles? Whose bright kids are these?
What happy family is this? In the kitchen two ice cream
sundaes sit on the counter. Those sundaes will never melt,
nor will they be eaten. The cookbook in the kitchen is
opened to a recipe for blueberry pancakes but in the living
room a bottle of wine and two glasses wait on a coffee table.
What time of day is it?

In house #17 I encounter the only joke on the lot: *Eat
More Pork* is stenciled on the side of a wooden chicken.

In house #12 it's Xmas.

In house #16 you've got a pastoral leitmotif in the prints
on the walls and the folksy bric-a-brac on the shelves. I
linger longest here. Outside I hear real church bells ring,
dull and somewhat muffled through the dense (R-41)
insulation. It's as though the bell is being clapped with a
cotton tongue. Through the window I see a wedding party.
I feel like a voyeur watching the bride and groom, inverting
the business of a Peeping Tom. I have to sneak up on regular
life. As much as rote irony informs my take on this,
I've been imagining living in these homes, where I'd plunk
one down, etc. What would I be able to see out my front
window? A wedding! In the master bedroom down the hall
the unwrinkled bed is empty, clean, without misery or
past. Happy love has no history and this bed is its home.
I'd like to come back some night and fuck in one of these
modular houses. The perfection is inviting but really I just
want to soil the sheets. I want to bring exhaustion into the

equation. All these houses are waiting for the future to come and haunt them.

I've overstayed. On my way out I stop in the kitchen. A plastic dinner is set on the counter. Tonight and every night in this home where time has stopped and there's no story or words we're having fake turkey, we're having fake carrots too, fake carrots and asparagus and baked potatoes with sour cream and chives, and afterwards, after this *tableau vivant* of bounty is cleared away, we'll grind coffee by hand in the wooden mill on the counter and serve it in the living room by the basket of logs for which, in #16 at least, there is no hearth.

Our boy will fall asleep on the rug and eventually I'll lift and carry him sleepily to the pine-log bed in his room, and after his prayers I'll tuck the quilt around his chin and tell him I love him.

Our girl will go to her room too, say her prayers too, beneath a picture of a roan horse, but in this case I'll only look on, from the doorway, as you bend to kiss her cheek.

Then you and I will go down the hall to sleep in that bed where no one's ever been before.

Brick Wall

Now what remains of the place is an anonymous wall of brick, but not so long ago my uncle ran a bar at 112 1/2 Clinton Street, the half being our family's share in the City of Big Shoulders, Chicago. If the Sears Tower were considered the gnomon of a sundial, and you were inclined to tell time by organizing shadows, then the bar was located at roughly ten o'clock in the morning. By midmorning the shadows swept in, the air darkened, and the streets turned silty, creating sunken rivers of early night, murky and unpromising to most people but suiting just fine the shady temper of the hardcore drinkers and gamblers the bar catered to. In fact they came precisely for that halfness, that demimonde aspect of the address. The building itself occupied an alley that had formerly served as a cattle run from the trains to the stockyards and packing plants on the South Side. Soon after the butchering ended, the bar opened for business. It must have been a big improvement not to taste blood in the wind, blown over the city from the slaughterhouses. When I lived in Chicago, those old abattoirs, long ago lost to history, had become inviolate and fixed in legend, but the city was changing again.

It was destroying itself, or sloughing off its old industrial self, and many of the brick warehouses and factory buildings in the neighborhood, gutted and windowless, deserted, were no better than caves hollowed from rock, with doors gaping open blackly, home to the homeless, the vast vacant interiors lit only by the light of fires burning in oil drums. In seeking the future a city like Chicago wrecks itself and returns to stone, at least briefly. There were piles of rubble such as you imagine in war, but the absence of declared enemies, and the lethargic unfolding of time, its leisurely pace, kept people from seeing the scale of the shift as catastrophic. Factories and warehouses and hotels, these old muscular hopes came down in heaps of brick and mortar, of pulverized concrete and cracked limestone, and then those cairns of rock, in turn, were cleared off to become barren lots as flat and featureless as the prairie they'd supplanted. Now brand-new buildings staunchly occupy those spaces, but for the duration, for the brief winter, spring, and summer I lived and worked next door to the bar, there was the constant gray taste of mortar on my tongue, my lips burning from the lime it was laced with, as clouds of dust were set adrift by each new day's demolition.

Brick is relocated earth, and the streets of a city like Chicago re-create a riverbank, in this case the clay banks of both the Mississippi and Ohio Rivers, where a good portion of Chicago's brick originally came from. The mining of clay is often referred to as "winning," a curious kind of victory, considering the clay used in brickmaking comes from the Carboniferous period, a subcategory of the Paleozoic, some 340 million years ago. Such a vast span of time would seem to temper any man's sense of triumph. It was during the Carboniferous that amniote eggs allowed ancestral birds, mammals, and reptiles to reproduce on land; flight was first achieved, too, as insects evolved wings. And then something happened, something happened to the birds and mammals and reptiles, to the nascent flying insects, to the whole ambition and direction of that geologic age. Everything died off and disappeared in that silent way only an eon can absorb and keep secret.

And yet with death the seedless vascular plants that existed in tropical swamp forests provided the organic material that became coal. These dead plants didn't completely decay and instead turned to peat bogs. When the sea covered the swamps, marine sediments covered the peat, and eventually intense pressure and heat transformed these organic remains into coal and shale. Curiously, burning brick in kilns only extends and completes the process epochal time itself used to form the source clay initially. Brick manufacturers use coal to fire and harden the clay, removing moisture and the last memory, the last vestiges of fluidity from the brick. (In fact there's a taxonomy of bricks based on how burnt they are: clinker brick, nearest the fire, becomes vitrified, glassy and brittle; red brick is the hardest and most desirable product of the kiln; and salmon brick, sitting farthest from the fire, is underburned and soft, unsuitable for exposed surfaces.) The obvious advantage of brick as a building material is that it's already burned, which accounts for its presence in Chicago after the fire of 1871. Brick transformed the city, ushering in an era of industrial greatness, completing—no, not completing, but extending—extending a process that began with a mysterious extinction, a vast unimagined loss.

During my time in Chicago my day job was to load cars and trucks with reproduction furniture, the historical imperative of which had vanished, vaguely, around the turn of the century. Nonetheless, shoppers from the suburbs drove to the city to browse the warehouse, its four floors and forty thousand square feet of fake antiques. They bought oxblood leather wingbacks, banker's lamps, baker's racks, oak iceboxes, old phones with a crank on the side that would, with a turn or two, summon the operator. The furniture was hokey, farmy, Depressiony. Of course none of the people who shopped the warehouse were cutting blocks of winter ice to haul by horse and wagon and then pack and preserve in layers of straw for the long hot summer. They lived in the suburbs; they had appliances.

It was curious and teleologically baffling. Why buy a phone you have to crank by hand when you can punch buttons to place your call? Why a wrought-iron baker's rack for men and women whose cookies and bread did their cooling at the factory? Why buy an antique that was hardly two weeks old?

The chaotic layout of the warehouse led many customers to believe they might, in some obscure corner, find a rare treasure, overlooked by others. But all this old stuff was absolutely brand-new; we carried special crayons in our pockets to keep it that way, coloring in the scratches before we showed people their purchases. These people wanted old furniture but perfect, they wanted antiques without time (the main ingredient and, you'd think, the very source of value in anything vintage). Still, the animating urge, the desire for the real, wasn't dead; the day I started the job I noticed nobody bought from the top, no one purchased the front item. Looking behind, for these people, equaled searching for the past, the authentic. Picky, savvy shoppers always made their selections by searching deep into the stacks and piles, mistrusting the surface, the present appearance of things.

Maybe nostalgia is a species of the ideal, a dream of a last interior, where all the commotion of a life is finally rewarded with rest, drained of history. We were selling the memory of something, of hard work and industry, of necessity, of craft and artisanship—the mendacious idea that life was gathered with greater force and organized in superior ways in the past. These faux antiques replaced the real past with an emblematic one. Or something. I could never quite untwist the riddle completely. When you stood in the warehouse the eye was pleasantly bombarded by a vastness filled. But the inspiration for most of the furniture we sold came originally from hardscrabble times, times of scarcity and unrest and an economy based on need, not surplus, and certainly not this absurd superfluity, this crazy proliferation, where two hundred oak iceboxes, stacked to the ceiling on layers of cardboard, would easily sell out on a Saturday afternoon. Why were people so avid and enthusiastic for the emblems of hardship? For what idealized interior could this possibly serve as honest décor?

After closing I'd slip a padlock in the loading-dock door, then stay inside: the furniture warehouse was also my home, I lived in there, vaguely employed as a nightwatchman. Every night I slept on one of, I'm guessing, two hundred sofas. I ate take-out dinners on tables that would be sold the next day. I read books by the greenish light of an ugly banker's lamp, set on a fake oak icebox. My boss was a man of great good fortune who liked to squire his mistress around town in a restored Model T Ford. He hired me to deter theft, set out glue traps, and hose down the dumpsters so bums wouldn't light the cardboard on fire, trying to keep warm. I simplified my job by rigging a cheap alarm system out of magnetic triggers and a hundred yards of lamp wire and a couple Radio Shack sirens perched on the windowsills. In the evenings I'd arm the thing by twisting together the exposed copper strands and head next door to my uncle's bar.

You entered the bar through a black door with a diamond peephole. There were nine stools covered in red leatherette. My uncle did book and collected numbers. Among the patrons you found a deep well of faith, a certain gut feel for what Catholic theologians would call analogical thinking, whereby you come to know the reality of God through signs. Gambling was how you negotiated the tricky path between situation and symbol. Winning was always an answer to a question. Most of the men were spooky about the stool they sat on and would rather stand all night than take a seat that had somehow been hoodooed by past bad luck. Many of these gamblers were afraid of the past, haunted by it, and this tilted their faith in the direction of fate, a less ample, less accommodating idea. On any given night thousands of bloated dollars would sit on the bar in wet frowning stacks. I'd never seen such sums. I drank Old Style and peppermint schnapps and lived off pork rinds and pickled eggs. The eggs floated in a gallon jar of green amniotic pond-water like specimens of some kind of nascent life-form.

Gambling and dim light and slow-rising smoke and the forgottenness of the place made it seem like everybody in the bar had strange and compelling mysteries behind them. They were dense with background, or so you inferred, or romanticized, because the present, the very surface of life, was so meager, so without evidence or account. In this sense my take on these men wasn't all that different from the way the warehouse customers saw our fake antiques. Any "background" I granted them was just another kind of décor, the décor of history, of image—in particular, history and image in their arrested or hardened forms, as nostalgia and cliché. The bar was the kind of place where people were "characters" and were known, to the extent that they were known at all, by some fragment of personality, a piece of self broken off and magnified until it was more recognizable than the original man behind it, overshadowing him. Character, in the bar, really was fate.

And so a character named Red Devil seemed a proxy voice, speaking for everybody, when he would cackle hysterically and yell out, "Mantina, 1963. I'm history!" Mantina was the state prison, but nothing beyond that was elaborated. To be history in America doesn't mean to be recorded, noted, added to the narrative, but precisely the opposite, to be gone, banished, left behind. To be history is to be cut from the story.

Other characters? Here are two. They even have character names, names I'd avoid if I were writing fiction: Al and George.

Al tended the bar at night. He'd been in the merchant marine and ate with a fat clunky thumb holding down his plate as if he were afraid the whole place might pitch and yaw and send his dinner flying. He was dwarfish and looked like an abandoned sculpture, a forgotten intention. His upper body was a slablike mass, a plinth upon which his head rested; he had a chiseled nose and jaw, a hack-job scar of a mouth; his hands were thick and stubby, more like paws than anything prehensile. Sitting back behind the bar, smoking Pall Malls, he seemed petrified, the current shape of his body achieved by erosion, his face cut by clumsy strokes and blows. His eyes, though, were soft and blue, always wet and weepy with rheum, and when you looked at Al, you had the disorienting sense of something trapped, something fluid and human caught inside the gray stone vessel of his gargoyle body, gazing out through those eyes. He was my only real neighbor. At closing he'd collect the glasses, wipe down the bottles, shut the blinds, and go to sleep on the bar. In the morning he'd fold his blankets and stow them away in a cardboard box.

George was another fixture in the bar, a salesman working, like me, in the furniture warehouse. He drank beer all day, chased with shots of peppermint schnapps so that his breath would smell fresh, as though he'd just brushed his teeth. Like most drunks he had the baffling notion he was getting away with it, fooling everybody. I felt sorry for George because he wasn't fooling anybody and couldn't see the truth, that he was being tolerated and temporarily ignored. With his insulin shots, instant coffee, his shabby dress, his elaborate comb-over, he led an obscure life, irregular and unobserved, except at the bar. There he gambled with a nervousness torqued up tight by a belief in the quick tidy fate of accidents, of moments that decide everything. Sometime in the past, he believed, things had gone wrong, gone fatally so. The present was his evidence. Divorce. Bankruptcy. Alcoholism. He had a gimpy leg, he was diabetic. He gambled the games, the horses, the numbers, the state lottery, everything. Sometime in the future there was a wager that would be won, a score that would redress everything, and perhaps this injection of faith, more than, say, a visit to the doctor, eased the pain for him.

"When I have money," he told me, "I can't sleep, I can't hardly eat. I don't feel good until it's gone."

In the bar a small bet was called "an interest bet," a wager that attached you fiercely, with greater vividness, to the flow of an otherwise monotonous day. It offered you a way into time, via the wide and democratic avenue of chance; even the smallest gamble instantly gave you a stake in the outcome of time itself. With a bet on, time had something to show you, held the promise of a revelation.

When George was betting he had the sensibility of a psy-
chotic, or a poet. There were nuances to assay, meanings to
consider. Accidents became auguries. The odds on unrelated
matters changed. Emotions rose to the surface, the buried
inner life became relevant, and he grew sensitive, tender,
his instinctual self, now resuscitated, engaged in the
world's new density. Nothing out in the actual world
demanded quite the same concentration of being, the same
focused energy. With money on the line, he became aware
of time, of his place in it, and planned ahead. On payday
he broke half his check into quarters, dimes, and nickels,
storing the coins in a coffee can at home; it was the only
way he could keep himself from gambling all his money
and make sure he'd have enough saved aside for food at the
end of the month.

Most people in the area around the bar were passing
through, transient. They were commuters who caught the
trains and left behind an acute emptiness, a hollow around
seven o'clock every night. Of course some people came in
search of precisely this lacuna, this moment when the day
lapsed into nothingness. Richard Speck sought it, holing
up at the Star Hotel a few blocks away, paying ninety cents
a night for his furnished room, in the weeks after he'd mur-
dered eight student nurses. This was 1966 and Speck
planned to hop a freight train west but never managed to

leave the Loop until he was sentenced to death. The single nurse who survived that attack, hidden flat beneath a bed, figured in my dreams for years. She squeezed herself beneath that bed and for hours listened to the sounds of sex followed by the sounds of death. I was a very young boy when this protohorrific crime happened but for some reason I know Speck tenderly asked the last woman he was raping if she'd wrap her legs around him. That winter they tore down the Star Hotel and I watched from a distance, watched the swing of a wrecking ball as it arced through the air, collided soundlessly, then came through, a couple seconds later, with a laggard explosion of crumbling brick.

At night black men in jalopy flatbeds scavenged through mounds of debris to save the bricks. In a book about brick, D. Knickerbacker Boyd writes: "When two bricks are struck together, they should emit a metallic ring." That's true. Bricks clink together with a satisfying ring akin to fine crystal. The sound has a clarity, a rightness. Bricks also improve with age and highly valued skids of cured Chicago brick were sold to people as far away as Phoenix and San Francisco, people who made walkways, garden walls, and barbecues from remnants of old factories. At night the air cleared of dust. To the west was Greek Town, across the freeway, with a row of restaurants concentrated enough so that some nights I'd pick up the arid scent of oregano; north was the Haymarket with its rotting fruit; and from somewhere, on certain nights, in a building

I searched for but could never locate, a candymaker spread the smell of chocolate and cinnamon in the air. From my window in the warehouse I'd hear the black men knocking away like moonlighting archaeologists, knocking until the old soft mortar was chipped loose and the clean red brick rang out as resonantly as a bell.

In the bar people kept drinking and betting right up to the very end. One night a stranger appeared and took George by the arm and led him gently, like a church usher, out to the sidewalk. Words were exchanged in pantomime. After a minute the stranger crushed George in the head with a length of pipe. George had raised his arms in supplication, beseeching, and when the pipe crashed down, his head bowed penitentially before he slumped to his knees, then fell forward on his face. You hardly ever see adults on the ground, they don't spin or twirl, they don't flop over and fall for the fun of it, not like kids. In my experience adults only went to the ground in death. George owed the man money. It was a confusing sight, seeing him like that, a grown man sprawled out on the sidewalk, small and broken, with no more control over himself than a child.

Now when I think of it, I understand it was never so much the potential for gain that animated gamblers like George, these men who had nothing, but being reawakened to a world where loss was once again possible. That's really what gave them life and drove them again and again to the game. Loss was their métier and to have that taken away, to be, finally, lost, was the worst thing imaginable. As long as you could fall farther you distinguished yourself from the fallen. Loss reinstated possibility, but possibility without hope. And perhaps this explains how all of us blithely imagined that the general wreckage would pass over the bar, that it was somehow exempt. Gambling offered a refuge from the outside world, its advances, its mysterious evolution. No one believed the bar would end, not because we didn't believe in progress, but instead, more precisely, because our kind of gambling, the wish of it, was an attempt to salvage the past. We weren't so much hoping to change the future as we were trying to amend history. We wanted the past completely restored and made livable. We believed that was the only kind of winning that counted.

Hell House

Hell House is a ramshackle arrangement of buildings meant to depict in a literal and somewhat medieval way the vast potential for ending up eternally damned. It's a haunted house in a haunted world, and through it you wind, down corridors of billowing black Visquine, through rooms luridly lit by strobes and TV screens, past stage sets peopled with rapists and murderers and terrorists until, briefly interred in a flat black coffin whose convenient and clever back door opens onto the afterlife, some souls ascend into heaven while most are dragged down to hell. It's an eschatological vision made up of a by-now-familiar triad of fundamentalism, outsized Texas bullshit, and some of the lowest conservative clichés about life in the big bad world—basically an undiluted version of our President, and as such, I guess, the potshots have already been taken. One hates to go to hell only to come back scoffing, but I took the tour three or four times, on two different nights, and the miscellanea of horror that made up this particular rendition lacked anguish and torment, not to mention the visceral, abreacted thrills you expect a good haunted house to have. There was a sort of moral hauteur that irritated me, but I was really hoping for spooky lowbrow sleights along the lines of peeled grapes for eyeballs and clumps of cold spaghetti for brains and whatnot. A major failing of Hell House was simply that it wasn't scary.

Physical fear is more immediately threatening than the far-off rumored torments of damnation, and Hell House might have found a more effective model had it based itself on the annual hazing of pledges and cadets or the ordeal of grunts at a Marine boot camp. I went to an all-boys school and for Frosh Week was made to sit in a tub of shit and lettuce, filled to the brim with fetid water and stirred with an oar, surrounded by crazed, shouting, doped-up seniors, and that was more unbearably nightmarish than any of the cornball lessons about moral hygiene I got from Hell House. Bodily fear just isn't rejectable, whereas moral and religious ideas, Pentecostal or Catholic, right or left, are better handled by hermeneutics than horror and anyway should operate under different rules of suasion. That conversion is sometimes accomplished brutally, and by subjection ought to be seen as aberrant and a sad lapse, a drop in the level of discourse. But hazing, with its disorientation, its deprivations, is fairly nondenominational. You don't need to evangelize in order to persuade. You confuse the senses, you tilt a floor, you dead-end a few of the dark corridors, you create prolonged silences, you flash white lights bright enough to blind, you blast noise so loudly stout men faint, you suffuse a room with the sulfurous reek of rotten eggs, you set up a gallery of yucky tactile experiences, you tease out a taste of eternity in a coffin with a claustrophobic stay in a closet, you do that and I really doubt the morality of abortion or homosexuality, for instance, would be half as worrisome, at least not for the immediate duration.

In other words, the argument of a haunted house ought to be aimed at the human body. In that sense, it should be morally neutral, or neutralizing. A good haunted house is about the utter collapse of our accidental differences, the uselessness of class, of gender, of education, of personal history, of all the distinctions we cobble together and call the self. Late enough at night none of this stuff protects you, not from the boogeyman. What's haunted or, more accurately, what's uncovered by terror, is the poor forked thing, and the agon of a haunted house isn't between God and Satan, or the righteous and the sinners, but rather between the self and annihilation. Horror resembles humor in its leveling capacity, although the anesthetic quality of comedy, its coldness toward bodily pain, is replaced in a moment of fear by a more complete and near-by peril. If comedy is somehow about the body as an unfeeling object, then fear is the surge of feeling into a body threatened with nonbeing. A haunted house poses ontological problems, and thus ought to place courage in jeopardy—it ought to reach down deep into the Platonic dualism between physical and spiritual courage and blast it apart. A good haunting gives us a workable vision of equality, a denominator similar to the *danse macabre.* It's probably fair to speculate that medieval depictions of putrefaction, particularly of worms crawling out of the bowels, drew inspiration from the visceral experience of fear, its locus in the upset stomach, which feels wormy when frightened, and to the extent that Hell House retained its folkloric roots it might have tapped that primitive seat of horror. A haunted house makes the experience of horror real, a thing inescapably participated in, with everybody hell-bound. But too often Hell House made the mistake of locating fear elsewhere, referring to moral arguments and social issues outside its walls and, in doing so, letting the drama of the endangered body drain away. Like it or not, a haunted house is a sensual affair, more like sex than theology, and won't survive too much abstract organization or the damping down of strangeness and intuition, of otherness or the mystery of skin or whatever. Hell House didn't obliterate distinctions and categories but erected them, the better to separate the saints from the sinners, at the expense of good fun. That a tour of hell would end in a call to prayer indicates the problem—if it had been more elemental and troubling, I would have come out the other end in need of water or air or sedatives.

Each room in Hell House could be considered a canto in the *Commedia*, particularly *The Inferno*, except that the idea of descent in Dante, the funneled shape of hell as you circle down into worse and worse sins, was ditched by Hell House in favor of a cosmologically flat canvas in which all sins were equally bad, and the entire trip instead resembled the morality plays and pageants put on for the feast of Corpus Christi in the fourteenth century. I'm not so much talking about design or construction here as the religious arrangement of sins. In that sense it stepped back from the Renaissance and the availability of perspective into the depthless stage of Everyman in the late Middle Ages. As a moral program, the schema for Hell House was linear, but as a physical structure, as architecture, it was anfractuous, like an intestine, twisting and turning, kinked here and there with knots, and the tour took you not so much down, as toward, an interior. It wasn't actually a house; it was more like visiting a sin zoo, strolling from room to room, watching the curious habits of fucked-up people. In each of the seven or so rooms you saw a playlet but there was no overall narrative. The entire visit lasted about an hour, but with no plot, no torquing up of the drama, I arrived at the day of judgment bored to death.

You were ushered through Hell House by ghouls in skull masks and black capes. Some of the ghouls wore tennis shoes and were obviously adolescent and their taunting had a certain playground aspect that was really annoying and bratty. There were even some especially short skinny ghouls no older than nine or ten or eleven who, relaxing between acts with their hoods off, came at me and the photographer as we dawdled behind our group, and told us to go to hell, pointing the way. Go to hell, they kept saying, over and over, obviously enjoying a curse that, for the two-week run of Hell House, was officially sanctioned. As the tour went on it became clear to me that these ghouls were quite specifically the voice of conservative values, although at first it had seemed as if they were supposed to incarnate the devil himself. Either way, these kids qua ghouls weren't giving off a full human vibration.

The tour took you through a variety of rooms, all staged like a theatrical set: the cabin of a jetliner, a rave, a hospital, a garage, a family room, a burial site, a cult sacrifice, a living room, a coffin, heaven, hell, and, before finally releasing you to the cold Dallas night and a cup of hot chocolate at the concession stand, a place to pray and perhaps even convert. Each room held its corresponding sin, the exact nature of which was often elusive. Loosely, you saw drugs plus sex, abortion plus sex, a slumber party plus sex plus murder, a cult sacrifice plus drugs plus murder, porno plus promiscuity plus bastardy plus sodomy plus suicide, and so on—there was a tendency to pile on and the impression was that you couldn't sin casually or recreationally but had to be hardcore and committed.

The audience watched as a group, from behind a cordon. A few examples should suffice to give a flavor of the whole. The set for the Abortion Scene was a hospital room. A girl in blue scrubs was wheeled in on a gurney, her crotch and thighs garishly soaked in blood. She screamed her head off while a doctor and nurse talked across the gurney, consulting so calmly and in such quiet voices they seemed to belong to another story entirely. Whoever wrote the script hadn't labored much over their dialogue—they showed no concern. You stared right at the girl's spread legs—I did, anyway—and that was weird. Her positioning sexualized the moment grotesquely—the bath of blood and the girl's agonal cries and even her death were an obvious but sick and grossly caricatured loss of virginity. More importantly, though, the girl's death was an act of revenge, it was retribution for killing an unborn child. It proved a conservative moral point—all the while she was dying the ghouls leaned over the gurney and ridiculed her.

The Slumber Party Scene involved two girls having a sleepover, listening to Mariah Carey, watching television and talking about what they want to be when they grow up. Then a man breaks into the house and abducts one of the girls, taking her to his car for what he calls "fun." You hear one of the ghouls say: "Don't you just love the smell of fresh meat?"—which totally threw off the point of view for me. Up to that moment my sympathy had been entirely with the girls, but now the ghoul seemed to be saying this young woman, hauled off to be raped, had somehow invited the moment, had transgressed, was blameworthy. Why else make this observation about fresh meat? It was creepy. Throughout Hell House it was mostly (sexual) girls who were in jeopardy, owing in part, I suppose, to the stock conventions of horror flicks; but the girls' bodies acted as territory in a disputed moral landscape. In the very next scene, which took place in a roofless structure, semi-outdoors, you saw the same girl roped to a joist, her hands tied above her head, while her abductor digs the hole he plans to dump her body in.

In the Porno Scene, we see this slumpy guy on a couch, watching dirty movies. His girlfriend comes home. She tells him she's pregnant. Then she tells him the child she's carrying isn't his; it's his best friend's. Then he violently forces some kind of humiliating sex on her. (We segue from the living room to the bedroom by watching a black-and-white video, quite blurry, that suggests rough stuff.) (The acting in these skits, by the way, was a mixed bag, ranging from okay to horrible, but many of the girls, when they had to scream, could really belt it out. It was never the scream of a real person in real pain but rather a homage to horror movies.) When the boyfriend leaves, the girl curses, giving out the very best, full-out scream of the whole tour, rolls on the floor, blasphemously accusing her Bible and God of abandonment, and eventually kills herself, simulating slashed wrists by popping a plastic ampoule of stage blood, quite convincingly, on her arm.

All of this was meant to be hideous and repellent, yet each room offered such a long, prurient, gazing look into the life of degradation that the scenarios often seemed like a spastic reaction against a real desire. I see two ways to take this observation. One is: somewhere along the line somebody had to imagine the act of sex, and that's one of the reasons, I think, that so many of the stories ended in murder—it was a way of punishing the imagination and paying for the fundamentalist sin of passing sympathy. The economy of it was creepy in its efficiency, with the condemnation and dispatch following so swiftly on the lapse or frailty or doubt, never considering, for instance, that promiscuity might be about an ambivalent need for love, or the desire, the stray hope, for something other than nothing—possibilities that would engage the imagination, tempting it. And two is: no one ever actually imagined any of this and Hell House was, instead, a gathering of clichés whose entelechy was fear and this house, far from being haunted, was in fact a safe refuge from the morally confusing universe out beyond the walls of black plastic. The sins were all childishly obvious, and I was aware, just vaguely, of being catechized. Very often I felt the tour wasn't about conversion but enlistment, and as such, it was a test of loyalty, with anyone who was the slightest bit recreant banished. Loyalty, in its darkest form, which left so much death as its legacy to the twentieth century, rids the divided self of anxiety and guilt, so that murder smiles. The ghouls in Hell House did a lot of gloating as others suffered.

There was a dispirited familiarity to the rooms, a lack of care about the shabby way things looked. Most of the furniture, I imagine, came from thrift stores, arriving at Hell House pre-saddened by other lives, other misfortunes. Everything lacked an element of choice, the memory of an original moment of hope about how things would be. The interiors were decidedly lower middle-class. The headboard in the porn scene was flimsy, not up to the rigors of a good sodomizing, and the vanity was one of those things that put you in mind of a wedding cake, white and elaborate and frilly, so vestal and princessy you just know heartbreak is in store for any girl still holding onto those misplaced hopes past the age of twelve. Things were sad as gesture, sad as furniture, in a world premised on the idea that appearance is a lie. The percale sheets, the sagging mattress, the framed art on the walls (because art is what a blank wall wants), all of it lacked vitality. The sofa was slouchy and vague as to color and the various easy chairs were worn and soiled and the carpet was the kind that's already there when you move in, with faint paths turned pale where other people have walked. It was a décor that suggested hope was elsewhere, in another life, and a décor that suggested unseen enemies, the sort of place that feels shameful and mean in a world where the failure to prosper is a sin. Of course, the sets were only meant to exist gesturally, as props, but there was something in the hard literal fact, in their mere presence, that encouraged you to see them in a realistic mode. The dingy and dim rooms made an atmosphere of sordid involvement—they were meant to indicate a shabby moral state, a despondency—but to me the "sins" did not seem moral so much as economic and aesthetic—a matter of both failed consumption and poor taste. Hopelessness had come to reside in the sofa on the porn set because it would never move again, because time had come for it and stayed, like an intimation of death. You felt nothing would change, that progress was gone and destiny mislaid; what the future held was repetition and sameness. There was a malignancy in this world, but it wasn't a problem you could blame on the devil. In Hell House it wasn't sin so much as sadness and despair and heartbreak and misfortune and cluelessness and just every stupid human possibility that was answered with damnation. People pathetically in need of help were shot.

And so wandering from room to room, every narrative ended in death, every story came to the same conclusion, until it felt as if a flawed and fallen world were finally being cleaned up and organized and made perfect. Mistakes were made, and the mistaken were efficiently condemned, leaving behind empty, squalid rooms in which it was impossible to imagine a tender unseen moment or kind word or a shared silence that wasn't murderous. It's perhaps needless to say, but the people in these skits lacked a living texture, were crude-minded and ugly in spirit and, in general, dismissively drawn. Hell House resembled big-time wrestling more than religion, a spectacle of types, overblown, exaggerated to the point of pornography with its parade of stock characters.

But Hell House was quite specifically somebody's vision of others. Whoever created Hell House despised people, their freedom, the varied possibility of them. Whoever it was could only imagine concluded lives, lives summed up by a single act, in a world where most of us have agreed, not always happily, to live with ambiguity. Every fundamentalism focuses on end-times, and Armageddon is, in a sense, a rhetorical trope, an emphatic and overwhelming conclusion, meant to wrap up and make tidy the mistaken wanderings of history. For a fundamentalist the end is one of the forms desire takes, a passion no different than lust or avarice, intense with longing and the need for fulfillment and relief. It's like they're horny for apocalypse. They only get off on dénouements, which is partly why Hell House never amounted to much more than a series of murderous conclusions. It only focused on that part of a story where life finds itself fated. Inside every act a judgment was coiled. Real people, with their ragged and uncertain lives, their stumbling desires, their bleak or blessed futures, would only break into the narrative, complicating the story, dragging it on, endlessly.

You would guess there'd be enormous anxiety involved in desiring the end since the end doesn't actually seem to be anything. And perhaps it's the messed-up management of this anxiety that accounts for Hell House's failure. Kierkegaard says anxiety "is altogether different from fear and similar concepts that refer to something definite"; he says "anxiety is freedom's actuality as the possibility of possibility." In other words, anxiety has no object; in fact it tries to become fear because fear has a definite object that can be faced with courage. I think it's fair to say horror bridges some kind of gap between fear and anxiety, using objects that are present yet unreal, objects that retain a somewhat objectless character. Horror makes visible the source of our anxiety, typically arriving dressed as death. It's nothingness in a black cloak, coming for all of us, a bequest of our bodies. But Hell House was premised on an antipathy to the suddenly helpless body, a hatred. It gutted the very thing that would make it compelling. Instead of indulging the thrills inherent to horror it swapped out anxiety for fear and came up with morality as an answer to annihilation. The hated content of Hell House was arrived at via a bunch of rejections, a denial, a suppression of the self, which helped the creator form a superiority over the rest of us who are slogging our way—living and loving, doubting and sorrowing—toward a hole in the dirt. The

Pentecostals who created Hell House converted their anxiety over the human body into persecution, and their horror set them dreaming of death.

Added up, room plus room plus room, Hell House was a holocaust. Everybody died. They died—they were killed off—because they lived the wrong way, made the wrong choices, believed and thought or felt the wrong things. The whole thing kind of sickened me. The last night I stood outside, absurdly thinking of Dante and his imagery, as the kids rehearsed their lines in the early dark before Hell House officially opened. Out on the lawn you heard a disembodied anguished call in the cold: "Where am I? What's going on?" And the strange music of a young girl warming her voice with: "God hates you. You killed your baby. I hear babies crying." I stood for a while in a field, listening, then went inside to inspect the Roscoe Fog Machine that would make Heaven the ethereal stuff of visions and the Styrofoam rock where, in half an hour, a sinner would be chained for eternity. The rooms lost nothing for being empty. In the hospital the blood-stained gurney waited for what the script called the Abortion Girl, a name as allegorical as Bunyan's Giant Despair. The sacks of plasma hung from their I.V. poles, the false charts were clamped into their clipboards, the stethoscope waited for its heart. The Abortion Girl would again scream and hemorrhage and die hideously a dozen or more times later that night, and again her nightmarish pain would be mocked, but for now an accepting silence held the room. In the Garage Scene, the paint cans, the hefty sacks twisted at the neck, the red car, all of it was stubbornly real in a way the stilted dialogue would not be. In the Slumber Party scene, soon enough, the raped girl would hang from her rope, the abductor would dig his hole. But the show hadn't begun yet and there was no morality just now. The shovel was there and so was the partially dug grave and the heap of overturned dirt smelled wet and loamy and the rope dangled, empty and waiting, as a light rain fell through the roof. It was beautiful, and a relief, mostly a relief, to feel the rain coming down and know how resistant reality was, how durable, even in a world drained of love.

Biosquat

In a story about paradise, the complications inevitably follow, so perhaps a simple description first—Biosquat is three or four acres of scrub, a derelict tract of land in east Austin (itself a somewhat neglected section of the city), on which Dave Santos has established at least the rudiments of an eco-village. There's a cattle gate and mailbox out front, and a forked tote road leads partway into the property; from there footpaths wind through stands of juniper and oak and mesquite. Plants in this part of the country, baffled by the sun, seek and hide from it all at once, suffering a kind of conflicted heliotropism in which the branches of a dry fissured oak, for instance, grow up and out, turn back, go down, curl and twist, writhing so much that, even still, they seem in motion, like the hair of a Gorgon. The heat in August is oppressive, and the umbrage these stunted trees provide is spotty, more shadow than shade, offering little relief. Underfoot, the blanched soil at Biosquat feels like crushed brick and hardly seems arable. I saw no wildlife other than a few lizards, although I was told rats and raccoons, as well as coral snakes, live in the area. Mosquitoes were plague-plentiful, and Dave Santos suggested, rather alarmingly, that the once numerous crows had been decimated by West Nile virus. In the distance you could hear the constant hum of cars, and while Biosquat's ambitions are somewhat Edenic, at present it still retains the mood and look of a vacant lot; it has a spurned and forgotten quality, as if the world had, without warning or explanation, fallen in love with someone else.

Once inside the gate, along the paths, you find the first improvements, the nets and tents and bamboo beds, the solar panels and the cistern and the terraced gardens, a limestone megalith surrounded by rickety scaffolds and a series of unfinished structures, the ceilings of which are fabricated from bike rims and a cladding of placards and signs left behind by old political campaigns. There's a pale green trailer and a toilet mounted on a tricycle and a trellis of unripe tomatoes hanging, again, from bike rims. There's welding equipment, there's rebar and conduit, there's an anvil on a stump and a primitive garden hoe cleverly forged from a piece of pipe and a chain ring. The visual impact of the place is surreal and collagist, although, sprawling with junk, it also comes quite close in character to the sort of illegal dump site every city has, those wooded hillsides that mysteriously fill with unwanted mattresses and shopping carts and washing machines. Over the couple of hot August days I spent at Biosquat, Santos often spoke of "trash worship," an idea meant to elevate debris into an aesthetic and invigorate refuse with a rarefied sense of social mission—something more high-minded and messianic than recycling, at any rate—and perhaps that's what he's up to, perhaps the bikes and the rebar and the bamboo aren't haphazard, aren't just old crap nobody else wants, but are instead the base materials for building the small, resonant civilization he imagines.

I, for one, was willing to believe. I was willing to believe that, on a warm fall night in the future, estivating frogs would bellow to life in ponds that, as of now, don't exist. I was willing to believe that human shit is second only to bat guano as a nutrient and fertilizer and that it's entirely odorless when mixed with mulch. I was willing to believe that a recipe of soybean oil and chili peppers would eradicate the mosquitoes and make for an edible pesticide. I was willing to believe in things I did not understand, in Hilbert space and eigenforms and combinatorics, and I was willing to believe in houses that would someday look, fantastically, like big puppets. I was more than willing to believe in a world in which, quite beautifully, nothing was outcast or lost or abandoned, not people or things or ideals. I was willing to believe in all the enthusiasms Dave Santos believes in—the radical circus and the mutant bikes and the chicken tractor and the gnat goggles and the flying robots and the car that runs on rain. I was even willing to believe, in principle, that an earthly paradise, lush and complete, could be improvised and sustained with rainwater, PVC pipe, a homemade cistern, and a solar-powered bilge pump. I was willing to believe all of this and more—that human migration and nomadism make sense, that pedaling a bike a mere six weeks a year will keep you in an eternal spring, that "Bucky Fuller" once bathed a family of four with a single cup of water—but I was not willing to believe this:

"Ultimately, I think colonizing the atmosphere is the solution to a lot of ecological problems. . . . [*Uh-huh.*][1] And it's also more sensible than the space fantasies—the idea that we're ready to build a bunch of rockets and blast off and live in orbit. [*Right.*] Engineering-wise, it's much simpler to colonize the lower atmosphere. [*Uh-huh.*] And so we have the stratosphere, is where I started theorizing. I lectured at UT Aerospace on the subject. . . . We could take carbon out of the atmosphere. We have excess carbon dioxide. We'd liberate oxygen to help us breathe up in the stratosphere. We could mix that oxygen in with our helium and live inside these huge cathedral spaces—we'd be talking a little like Donald Duck, but because of the solar energy coming in, we'd have a shirtsleeve, close-to-sea-level-pressure environment, up above the weather [*Uh-huh.*],

1. My questions and exclamations—every noise I made—appear here within brackets.

and totally reliable electric solar power. [*Yeah.*] And we could use that electricity for ion propulsion to crack the carbon dioxide, to regenerate the ozone, using the catalytic reactors of these ion-propulsion engines, and get carbon credits, from, like, the nations that want to do something good for the environment. We could build this aerial civilization from the carbon we've dumped in the atmosphere. [*Yeah, yeah.*]

"And then go anywhere we want, like the round-the-world ballooners. By knowing, by being able to visualize the atmosphere, they can steer [*Uh-huh.*], and they don't even have any propulsion except the ability to go up and down. [*Right. Right. Right, right.*] So we have these sites around the world that are like stratospheric elevators, where prevailing winds hit a mountain and create a stratospheric mountain wave, and so those are places you could have gliders that soar up to your stratospheric cities. [*Yeah.*] Getting down's easy. [*Right.*] You could just sky-dive. [*Uh-huh.*] Out of the stratosphere. [*Yeah, yeah.*] It would be the basis of an Olympian civilization, living up in the clouds. I'd like to see socially conscious hippies get there as opposed to some death star. [*Yeah, yeah, yeah. So you see Biosquat in relation to everything you're saying as . . .*] As a stepping-stone. [*Yeah. It also seems somehow, uh, it seems very fluid.*]"

———

Dave Santos has some higher education, but essentially he's a kind of autodidact. He went to Washington College ("a party school on the great waterbird migratory flyway of the Chesapeake"), dropped out, enrolled at the University of Texas, dropped out, matriculated, dropped out, where-after he cut tuition costs by auditing classes or simply sitting in on lectures that interested him. ("I was able to lap up aura and knowledge from Nobel Laureates and other legends in this way.") In conversation, he has that ravenous fierce range of the self-taught: ion propulsion, Foucault, Hazlitt's translation of Montaigne, heuristic programming, Rousseau in the original French ("It wore me out."), matrix algebra, zines, Mircea Eliade, Radio Shack manuals, predicate calculus, pamphlets on composting. Without much lingering or elaboration, the learned references pile up—some Foucault here, a little Rousseau over there—in an allusive, jumbled analogue to the vacant lot Biosquat is built on. For Santos—fringy, wandering outside the codes and canons of academe—every book he's read is a perfect, remarkable *objet trouvé*, to which he brings tremendous zeal.

Like a lot of autodidacts, Dave Santos wants to out-smart you. At times his use of language sounds impressively academic but forged, like a false passport. He favors, for instance, coinages ("biobikes," "edjidotopia"), as if he were exploring the frontiers of a discipline, working a lonely terrain and discovering things for which, as yet, there are no names; or he dresses up a phrase for the scientifically credible sound it will make ("Arrest Proofing Protocols," "Bivy Head Observatory"); and whenever there is an opportunity to swap in a complex word for a simple one, an elaborate construction for a clear explanation, Santos is there, substituting "rear-optics" for "mirror," "microhedonics" for "good fun," and "dive reflex" for "hitting the ditch," creating his own taxonomy, a systematics behind which, I suspect, there is no system.

This makes him powerful and persuasive to a point, and never less than fascinating, but I think too that his showy, protesting intelligence masks an insecurity, a feeling, never entirely put to rest, that he doesn't belong in the room. He talked about attending AI conferences with his home-built robots and being "respected by these people who, normally, without a Ph.D., you shouldn't even be in the same room [with]." "Shouldn't" is a curious choice—why not the more neutral "couldn't" or "wouldn't"?—in that the word subtly switches the speaker: it doesn't actually belong to Santos but to the voice of an absent, unnamed, scolding authority. Here, then, is the central theme of paradise—banishment and exile.

And so in exile—let's say—he elaborates his own thing. The various structures at Biosquat include the sleeping quarters, mostly tents and mosquito netting, and "the mother ship," as Santos calls it, a travel trailer the color of canned peas that sits under a roof. The trailer is rough and shabby, the kitchen kind of a sty, ruling out any chance that Biosquat has any hidden desire for conventional, uptight domestic order. All of this is fairly standard, and the cheap, sagging tents in particular give the place the familiar look and feel of a homeless camp. The chicken tractor is interesting—a low cage laid out along a footpath, with a plywood coop at one end. The idea is that the chickens, confined to a run, will peck and till the earth, kill the weeds, eat the insects, shit and thereby fertilize the soil, but just before I arrived they had been depredated by raccoons and dogs (dramatizing a flaw in the curious harmonic stasis of Eden that I could never resolve in childhood: what would everybody eat, I'd wonder, if they couldn't eat each other?). A homemade cistern collects water from the roof of the carport; the water is then pumped to the terraced gardens, and a solar oven sitting on a shopping cart—a corolla of petal-shaped panels open to the sun—generates just enough heat to cook a pot of beans.

The most interesting structures at Biosquat are built with an armature of bike rims sheathed with corrugated plastic. The rims are fastened together with tie wire and arch nicely toward the sky, propped up from below by lengths of bent rebar and the trunks of scavenged trees. The chrome spokes make for exactly the kind of airiness Santos seeks elsewhere through elevated language; their thinness gives an otherwise stout ceiling a delicate appearance and, clad with the corrugated plastic, which is predominantly white, the rims and spokes together look, overhead, like a drove of gauzy parasols. The curving shape and the texture of the skin remind you of Gehry, as does the collagist sensibility and the use Santos makes of cheap-tech materials. At this point in their construction, somewhat unfinished, you feel like calling these ingenious, junky, Quonset-like things "pieces"—as you would a piece of sculpture. It's one of the paradoxes I found most intriguing about Santos that he's a commissioned sculptor, working in an art bound to materials and materiality, while putting such a heavy, personal accent on ideas of ascent and the ethereal. This isn't an ambition foreign to sculpture, for sure, and even straight verisimilitude is an attempt to lift life out of stone, transcending a basic, obdurate fact about the physical stuff. So the pieces are unfinished—although given their resemblance to collage and their use of trash, they may always resist looking finished—and in their present condition encapsulate the cosmology of Santos's project as a whole. There's the empyreal ceiling above, shaped like a parachute, and then, below, Santos is building rude walls from red clay that he digs out of the ground; in between, the walls will be reinforced using, of course, bike frames— a sort of colorful bike rebar that, at this point, remains exposed, so that the bikes emerge from the clay and sit at a sort of midpoint between earth and sky.

———

Flight is a leitmotif for Santos, and the theme reaches richly into all the word's meanings, from flying to fleeing to the exuberances of fancy and transcendence to joyrides and quests. "You need that metaphoric inspiration to get a focus," he says. And so when he talks of nomadism, the idea veers from roving bikes to migratory birds and eventually melds into "a dream of autonomous migration in self-sufficient skybikes with ultralight amenities. It is a soaring of light spirits—dematerialized, floating, ethereal, intense." A skybike probably should not "dematerialize," not in flight, anyway, but it's the turning of this kind of trope that marks for me the line between belief and disbelief, between accepting the visionary and balking at the vision. The movement from skybikes as an engineering feat to light spirits as a condition of the soul is purely metaphoric. It owes more to the Book of Revelation than it does to physics, more to the ecstatic tradition in poetry than to aeronautics. Looking around Biosquat, at the tangle of bikes or the hardscrabble soil, the effort of translating stubborn matter into an immaterial vision is evident. It's slow going. And while the freedom described here is a spiritual event—an apotheosis—it's also an escape from the poverty of the corporeal world, a gripe you always hear from lyric poets, saints, and visionaries.

This is tricky terrain, the transition from the airy intensity of the imagination to the denser inspissations of reality. In his writings on the Web, Santos so often leaves sense for sound, so often eases away from the meaning of a word for the music it will make and abandons practicality for the pleasing image, that his real project seems to be about the liberation of language, about words loosed from their context, about poetry. (In a passage I really like, he writes that the pilots of these skybikes "use dust devils as the lift of last resort. You kamikaze into them, treetop high, and hope to rise enough to catch a big convection cell. . . . Too big, you dement into a winged blue Popsicle.") In this context, Santos reminds me of the French utopian Charles Fourier, and both men are closer to the *furor poeticus* of Plato than they are to a hard-minded historian like Marx or a more sober utopian like Robert Owen. Fourier believed the world would eventually contain 37 million poets equal to Homer, 37 million mathematicians equal to Newton, and 37 million dramatists equal to Molière— although, he admitted, these were only "approximate estimates." He believed there were 810 psychological types and organized his *phalanstère* to include two of each, a man and a woman. He believed in nearly complete sexual liberation—sodomy, homosexuality, pederasty, bestiality, fetishism, and sex between close relatives—and he also believed that salt would one day leech from the seas and that those seas would in turn become oceans of lemonade.

———

Some of what Santos is up to might be called Art Brut, although in its American form, as Outsider Art, its appreciation contains a quotient of irony and class snobbery or condescension that has always bothered me. Plus, Santos doesn't qualify strictly—too much training, as a sculptor and muralist, and too much savvy, too much awareness of his renegade role in relation to the gallery world. He's something of a pisser, resistant to art rather than naively unaware of its trends, so perhaps the uppercase label that suits him best is Marginal Art. At any rate, Biosquat has some of the Art Brut stuff—its materials are humble, it's the work of a solitary devoted soul, it's eccentric and enigmatic, it's being undertaken in near total disregard of public opinion—and may one day resemble the Watts Towers or the Palais Idéal. Biosquat is packed with thought, textlike, and its themes—cycling, nomadism, trash worship, solar power—touch everything from the fences to the toilets. The toilet I used, for instance, is your traditional white porcelain seat mounted on a trike, and when you're done, you toss in some mulch (not lime, which, Santos says, just turns the waste into a bunch of brick turds), and then periodically the whole contraption is inched forward, leaving in its trail a swath of fertilizer suitable for gardening. In a couple of places around the property, there were also pissoirs fashioned out of plastic Clorox jugs, from which the bottoms had been snipped, and black hoses that then ran into beds of wood chips, the exact agro-purpose of which escaped me, but had something to do, I imagine, with urine's acid content. The emunctory enthusiasms of people in eco-villages, always fiddling with their waste, might make for an interesting study, but meanwhile the tricycle toilet at Biosquat worked wonderfully. It didn't stink at all, a claim I'd seriously doubted when Dave Santos first mentioned it, and crapping alfresco is always nice.

One of the laws of Biosquat, it seemed, was that nothing could be what it was originally. The gnat goggles were made from the screens of a tea infuser; to the fat ends of a set of chopsticks Santos had fixed, on one, a tablespoon, and on the other, a toothbrush. He called this general category of transformation "mutant technology." Some of these transformations—particularly the bikes—are right in the grain of a particular brand of American genius that flourished in the years following World War II. This genius centered around car culture, and the era probably reached its meridian in Southern California in the 1950s and 1960s, waning somewhat by the 1970s. Dave Santos isn't all that different in spirit from a SoCal gearhead like Ed "Big Daddy" Roth, automotive designer and visionary, creator of Rat Fink, who pioneered the use of fiberglass in car bodies and was a guru/hero to the legions of boys who built scale models of his hot rods—the Outlaw, the Beatnik Bandit, the Mysterion—and any shade-tree mechanic who had an aesthetic bone aching in his body. Roth was celebrated in Tom Wolfe's seminal early essay "The Kandy-Kolored

Tangerine-Flake Streamline Baby," and even today his legacy of transformed, souped-up, mutant machines hasn't entirely gone away. The idea of an utterly transfigured kick-ass car is still amply evident among the Hispanic boys who cruise Hollywood Boulevard on Friday nights, although in the main that lexicon has gone out of the life of white kids (those who don't live in Barstow or Bakersfield or Stockton, anyway).

Now autoshop's dead, and probably hipsters study art, anyway, but back in the day a certain, perhaps limited manhood made its way into the public by lovingly (and literally) deconstructing one of the culture's main givens—the car—and metamorphosing it with saws and torches, complex paints and layers of lacquer, until it shed its dull utility and became art—primarily, as Wolfe says, sculpture. (Roth cast the bodies of his bizarro cars with plaster molds.) It's no accident that this kind of revamping flourishes in macho cultures, since it's so openly about the male need for outlets of sensitivity that aren't permissible and are, in fact, studiously removed from spectacles like football. In an essay quite similar in gist to Wolfe's, Dave Hickey argues that hot-rodding is about dissent, which I think is partially true. Hispanics in L.A., for example, often favor hopped-up trucks, in part to recoup and then triumph over the denigrations of migrant labor life, spent riding around dusty fields, packed in the backs of pickups like loads of produce. The very qualities that make a truck functional for farmwork—beefy suspension, extra clearance, and so on—are completely subverted in a lowrider, which couldn't handle even the slightest rut without high-centering or fatally bashing the rocker panels. Lowriders are so outrageously spiffy and cool—a new dandyism—they look like they've never done a day of work in their lives.

And just so, Dave Santos's bikes are ridiculous from the standpoint of utility. Everything Lance Armstrong (also from Austin) might want for the Tour de France—lightness, strength, balance, low resistance—is out the window once Santos fires up his torch and begins to build a mutant bike for his migratory trips to Mexico: lengthening the seat tubes by a couple of feet, raising the bottom brackets, setting the chain rings and cranks on a vertical axis, chopping the forks, making the saddles cushy with wads of foam and a wrap of duct tape, improvising fairings of plaster and fabric. They aren't conventionally beautiful, these bikes, and they don't even seem roadworthy—they're circus bikes for goofy, toppling clowns—but in their strange, abstracted state they're definitely objects, maybe sculptures. Everything Dave Santos does at Biosquat is an attempt to render a vivid interior external, and as such, his bikes are primarily an index to the visionary mind of the maker. But the problem with any visionary experience, plaguing all seers, is one of verification. I'm not talking about vision as an eyeball thing (did you see that?), but vision as imagination, intuition, revelation (did you experience that?), where issues of authenticity, truth, and validity (are you nuts?) become hugely problematic—for example, when you're talking about winged bikes, fitted with feathers of old, still utile trash, that might one day carry hippies to the stratosphere.

At one point Santos said he was fascinated by "those little golden ages that are gone before you know it." But he also said: "That's where I'm a little pessimistic, because sometimes cultures reach a peak and they don't just keep on going forever, you know—then there's ruins and thousands of years, and, you know, after ancient Greece, they had a lot of downtime, the action went somewhere else. So there's a lot of sadness, a lot of missed opportunities, a lot of mistakes." Biosquat aspires to get outside this story. It's an attempt at creating some kind of suspension, anyway— a world of signs and wonders, of marvels and revelations, of continuous amazement. Every object at Biosquat is tinkered with until it's an original, toyed with until it resembles nothing else. Even Santos's fondness for neologisms is a way of wrenching old words into something new and unique. I'd never seen a toothbrush on a chopstick—it's so Dada and sensible at the same time—nor had I taken a shit on a trike. Each object—like Big Daddy Roth's hot rods or the Hispanic boys' chopped and channeled trucks—is an attempt to seize life at a moment of glory, to embody an essence and hold it, stilling the ephemeral, apotheosizing what would otherwise pass, as all things pass. The mutant bikes, the bamboo beds, the gnat goggles, the Chicano robots, and the corrugated-plastic domes are all singular—freaky, a one-off, an aberrance, a whole world of exceptions. All of it exists somewhere beyond sadness or mistakes or missed opportunities, because, transformed, there's nothing to compare it to. It's meant to speak to you in the language of the burning bush, it's supposed to be a walk on water, it's all truth of another order, like the coin Christ pulls from the mouth of the fish to pay the temple tax. These are called miracles, of course, and they break a lot of natural laws, but as transformations, utterly singular, beyond argument, they too are meant to convince you that the kingdom has already arrived, here on Earth.

Orphans

The intent of a façade is exoteric but there are obvious problems with that. While in St. Petersburg, for instance, I stayed for several days at the Moscow Hotel. That particular exterior does the work of a façade, presenting a warren of windows so relentlessly uniform the eye is baffled and ultimately rejected; from a distance, you can't quite locate the entrance. But if, from outside, you can't find a way in, from inside, especially walking the hallways, you can't imagine a way out. The interior space is made of incredibly long, horrid corridors lined on either side with black doors like answers to a question you'd long ago forgotten. You feel exhausted, seeing such a dreary path ahead of you on the way to your room. You begin to feel the life behind any one of the black doors will do, any future, any destiny. Once inside, your room, it turns out, is only the imitation of something nice, an arrangement of resemblances.

And probably the most esoteric Russian encounter is with a woman seated inside a glass booth. You look through thick Plexiglas, you speak into a small vent or round hole, and the grim interior light from a low-watt lamp, the dull brown walls, the sense of the woman as someone seated at the bottom of a box, all of this seems to encourage her indifference, embolden it. Everything inside—the adding machine or cash register, the telephone, the woman's lips—looks antiquated. You may want to exchange money or call a cab or simply make an inquiry, but you are clearly intruding on an isolation that's sanctioned or bolstered, somehow, by an official boredom. What sense of desire or anticipation can you expect from a woman locked away like this, limited to such a small, immobilizing space? It seems to be a matter of perfect indifference whether or not you have rubles to spend or the question you want to ask is ever answered. It's like tricking a troll, hoping for passage. If you can consider a façade the blank face, then the woman inside the glass booth is the hardened heart, neither of them inclined to charm. Their efficacy comes from elsewhere. You can't imagine the liberation of such a woman, from either her booth or her boredom, and the information you're after is isolated too, like a dwindling, rationed commodity, lacking market efficiency and flow. In my limited experience, you never came away from one of these occult encounters with enough of what you were after. The arrangement is tightfisted, as though ideas and information weren't meant to circulate, as if they could actually be contained inside what amounted to aquariums. You look into that glass booth enough and what you begin to see, I imagine, is your own soul.

Or whatever—but I'd felt somewhat pixilated from the moment I stepped off the plane in St. Petersburg. The international airport there's no better than an American bus station, small, dingy, bleak, with that strange lassitude that seems almost the opposite of travel, as if no one's really going anywhere. Somebody was supposed to meet me, and I lingered around this dreary green lobby, reading and rereading the placards people were holding up, but none of the signs had my name written on it. It occurred to me I might call the woman who was supposed to pick me up. In my pocket I had just a crumpled dollar. I talked to one woman in a glass booth who couldn't tell me how to use the phone, and another, obviously distressed woman, also in a glass booth—the information booth—who was hiding beneath a shelf and would not raise her head up and talk to anyone, let alone explain to me how to use the phone. I kept walking over to the wall where the telephone was mounted and staring at it. It looked exactly like a phone but it might as well have been a confounding objet d'art. I went outside and sat. The air was gritty with particulate matter, dust blown in from the barren fields surrounding the runways. It was hard to tell if the airport was under construction or being dismantled. Pieces of metal sheathing flapped in the wind, and the fences meant to cordon the work areas were falling down. A sign gave "apologies for the inconveniences connected with terminal reconstruction." Back inside I found yet another woman in yet another glass booth who sold phone cards. Eventually, outside, I managed to make a phone work and I called my contact, who said she was so sorry, she thought I was arriving tomorrow, but for roughly 1,500 rubles, I could easily catch a cab to the Moscow Hotel.

More than money, what I needed was rest, at the very least to quell the misgivings I had been having about my role as a writer. On the transatlantic leg of the flight I had sketched out a bunch of alternatives: I mulled over writing in the urgent voice of a liberal reformer, or expressing a stoic world-weariness, or getting riled up and angry in an exposé, or working toward a generous-spirited puff piece. These were all stories I thought about telling. And then on the plane from Frankfurt to St. Petersburg I was fated to sit beside a couple from Cleveland who'd come to Russia to adopt an eight-year-old girl. The girl, they told me, had been abandoned by her family, which the man attributed to the shift from a "communistic to a capitalistic society." He said this quite emphatically. In fact he was an emphatic person the way other people are tenors or baritones, and because I had the window seat and felt trapped I began to get buggy. Everything he said stuck to my skin. He asked a lot of questions that were aggressive and blunt and designed to elicit or provoke simple yes or no answers. It wasn't a conversation; he was just beating the air like a rug, hoping to knock all the doubt and ambiguity out of it. I kept wondering—strangely—if he was an *avocat*—I mean I wondered if he was a lawyer, using the French word in my head. All three hours of the flight I felt like I'd been locked away in an interrogation room. There was hardly any space for me in the sturdy architecture of his conversation, and yet this man planned to adopt and house a child.

His wife seemed kind and sweet and obsequious, with a soft chin that marred her real chance at beauty. Every time I looked at her face I felt lost. She had that bright-eyed, very dull niceness well-meaning people often have that strikes you as full of shit until you realize there's nothing behind it. It's real. She was nice. When she asked about my business in Russia I was totally incoherent, and once her husband, the avocat, sniffed me out, he really started hammering the air with questions. Now I was on trial. I became almost spastically inarticulate and confused and couldn't describe what I was doing in a satisfactory narrative style. By the time we landed, my business had become a shame to me, a fault of mine; I was guilty. They, on the other hand, had a story whose somewhat gooey mucilage was goodness, this couple from Cleveland. I'd just read about this very thing on the plane from Chicago to Frankfurt, pouring over a learned article on attachment disorders and the developing mind—my sister thought it might be relevant in observing orphans—in which the author talked about some guy named Grice and his four maxims of discourse: "1. quality—be truthful and have evidence for what you say; 2. quantity—be succinct; 3. relation—be relevant or perspicacious, presenting what has to be said so that it is plainly understood; and 4. manner—be clear and orderly." Supposedly violating any one of these precepts indicates mental problems, and I'd just hashed all of them. But the couple from Cleveland were like Grice apostles. That's why they were adopting a child: they had a story in mind.

It was with a feeling of relief, then, that I made it out of St. Petersburg, five hours by two-lane road, to Svirstroy. At the orphanage, bare-limbed birch trees lined the driveway leading to the front door. Snow was still on the ground, patches of snow drifted into the protecting shade of pine trees, even though at this time of year, in May, the sun wasn't setting until after eleven o'clock at night.

Within an hour of my arrival a couple different kids, independently, asked when I was leaving. It seemed a strange question, out of sequence, but the defining fact of these kids' lives, I would realize, is the transience of adults. A lovely, soulfully sweet girl named Tonia told me her history in epochal blocks marked by the passage of adults, like a dry account of royal succession. Up till seven she lived with her mother and father, from eight to nine she lived with either friends or her aunt, from nine to eleven she lived with her grandmother, who died of stomach cancer on August 19, 1995—the way Tonia mentioned the exact date seemed salient in a life lived largely without celebrated days. Anyway, deep down there must be huge anxiety about departures, and the question, I came to understand, was meant to allay a real fear about the fragility of adult relations. What the kids wanted to know was how much of their interest they should invest in me, another ghostly passing adult—in other words, what's the rate of return on caring?

A boy named Kosta bluntly told me I wasn't staying long enough to write anything, and when I asked how long he thought I needed, he said three months, a year. He wasn't being cutting or cruel or defensive, just thinking about and weighing the world, his world, after all. One afternoon I went to the village and bought hot dogs and bread, catsup and mustard, pop and cookies, and about fifteen of us lit a big bonfire on the banks of the river and had a picnic. By the way, none of these kids goldbrick or grouse when it comes to work. They have chores at the orphanage, and when it came time to gather wood for our fire, suddenly and without a second prompting it was madness—they hopped to, hauling branches and logs and sticks and arm-loads of dry grass, and we had our fire blazed up in minutes. But after we'd eaten and were lazing around, watching big ships haul raw logs upriver, a beautiful boy, Maxim, smiled and said, "That was good food, but it's over. Write it down. Write it down in the magazine." The comment stuck with me. Like everyone, I tend to think things that last have greater value than passing moments, and on some level, too, I was probably condescending to the kids. I thought I was treating them to something they'd not soon forget. On both counts Maxim, in a frank, simple, cynical way, was putting things in perspective for me—his perspective.

The orphanage was built originally as housing for pilots-in-training, and for several years after World War II it held German and Hungarian prisoners, some of whom, across an open field, are buried and memorialized in a grove of trees. A couple years ago some old people came, the kids told me, and cried. This seemed to mystify them, how people would remember each other, and especially the dead, over such a vast stretch of time. You imagine, of course, that the prisoners buried behind the orphanage perhaps left orphans themselves, and that these old people, on a final pilgrimage, might well have been visiting their fathers. The kids' comments captured a certain—I won't say block-age—but a dreamy remove from a reality that would be fairly pedestrian for most people. It would not be the last time I noticed this sort of loose drift in their associations, an ellipsis in the mind that helped them slide over rough terrain in their history.

At the edge of the orphanage property are what the kids call the red ruins and the black ruins, and I was taken on a tour of both, each interior with the same dust, the same broken slant of light, the same weeds and rubble and cracked glass, but the black ruin is a former bomb shelter dug deep into the ground, and the red ruin, a brick building aboveground, seems once to have housed a repair shop of some sort—there were steel doors of outsized proportions meant to allow the passage of trucks. In the red ruin padlocks remained on doors without hinges, and wire bars gated windows without glass. The ruins mainly suggest a kind of contrapuntal relation to the orphanage itself, which dates from the same era yet still stands. In America, looking back, we don't really arrive at history so much as we enter romance, some place of eternal beginnings, but here, even in the bucolic Russian countryside, the devastations of war are marked by dead prisoners, shelters, stone defilades and, deep in the woods, what I took to be bomb craters—suspiciously odd declivities in an otherwise smoothly rolling or flat landscape. Here, there are ruins, and then there are things saved from ruin, things that escape, and the difference is emphatically alive and real, even if you can't calculate why by using the ungovernable terms of historical destiny.

Maybe more than the building itself, the land around the orphanage and the elaborate network of footpaths create for the kids a sense of place. There are trails through the birch and pine, across fields where, every spring, the kids burn leaves and work the ash into the soil and plant potatoes, trails that lead to the river, to the school, to the village, to ponds and creeks and springs flowing up from beneath the ground with cool, drinkable water, trails that are a story in themselves, worn by wandering feet over fifty years, worn by joy and hope and habit and need, trails like a sentence spoken, each a whisper about the surrounding world, a dialogue with doubt or desire that's ultimately answered by a destination. Many of the children have either no history or a severely foreshortened sense of the past, but these trails, worked into the grass or through the forests by others before them, send the kids off to play in a shared world—shared not just in physical space, but down through time. It must in some humble way ease the isolation, like Crusoe finding a footprint in the sand.

Time and a lot of touching have turned the interior of the orphanage funky, with a lived-in feel that now will likely never go away—it's there in the worn wood, the marble steps chipped or cracked so long ago that the original sharp, jagged wounds have since been smoothed and cicatrized like a weal by countless passing feet. The paint on the railings is layers thick, the broken windows are patched but not replaced, the tiles that peel up remain missing. Things inside were so worn and rubbed and handled by living beings that the interior had lost a lot of its rectangularity, and was replaced, instead, by a roundedness, a kind of inner burrowed shape arrived at by working the materials from within, like the nest of a wren. I found this fascinating, and loved discovering touches of it, combing the place for evidence of the tide of children, the softening action of them against the hard surfaces and correct angles favored by the original architects. Doorsills were scooped like shells by scuffling kids, and the jambs, at various heights, had lost their edge as lingering children held them, dirtied them, and picked at them until they had to be repainted, over the years, with many quick coats of high-gloss enamel. The stone floors held smooth undulations where the kids habitually walked, wearing troughs that you could feel by skimming your feet across them and that you could see, in certain lights, as a rippling reflection. Heavily trafficked areas of the orphanage received the most paint, so the lower walls had a receptive, accepting density, an imperfect but pliant look, and the railings on the stairwells, though made of metal, looked as though they'd been recently dipped in hot caramel.

The kids live in spacious, decent rooms with high ceilings and big windows. The boys pasted stuff to the walls—ads for cars torn from magazines, or pictures of German rock stars ripped from the newspaper—and scrawled a little graffiti with black felt pens—in other words, pretty much a rendition of a boy's room in America, but without the wherewithal. In one of the rooms, a hole had been punched in the wall, through the plaster and lath, which the boys used to communicate with the kids in the adjoining room. That it was unsightly didn't bother them one bit. They called it their telephone. These same boys later showed me their pet rats, and at the base of a plywood divider meant to keep males and females separate, the rats, too, had begun to gnaw a hole into the next room. I can't wring a dark poignancy out of the comparison between rats and orphan boys, however, because Svirstroy just wasn't that way. What the boys did wasn't vandalism, it wasn't destructive or ornery. If anything, the hole in the wall was a rough, clumsy modification the kids made because they're extremely close to one another. They'd restructured the building to suit their needs; that hole in the wall was about their hope for love. It may have looked destructive, but it was really an act of restoration. In general, boys and girls alike sought each other out, they sought and found proximity, and no one seemed at all defensive about his or her space. This seeking was one of the more noticeable aspects of my stay there. Relaxing on the lawn or sitting by the river, the kids would naturally clump up, pillowing their heads against each others' bellies, a whole chain of children in a circle, all quite free and unguarded about touching.

In an American institution the general disrepair might be seen as signs of decrepitude and disintegration, of a shoddy slide, but the direction at the orphanage seemed quite the opposite, upward, integral, a sense of pieces coming together. The clinical rectitude that serves us so well in America might also prevent us from doing the human thing in some cases, and I can't quite imagine an old building, owned by the government, turned over to the care and maintenance of kids; the impulse would probably be quashed by the obstacles. We'd have to knock Svirstroy down and haul it away in pieces before we could begin. In an obliquely related theme, my whole time at the orphanage I could never find any wastebaskets; my pockets filled with trash. In America, of course, every public hallway has a rich battery of waste-disposal options, with separate receptacles for newsprint, pop cans, apple cores, or whatever. For obvious reasons, poor orphan kids don't generate much garbage. Generally, their present doesn't obsolesce and convert into the past quite as rapidly as it does for kids in America; there isn't the abundance, and in the absence of a steady stream of the new, stuff doesn't get used up and sloughed so easily. (The boys, for instance, hoarded batteries for their Walkmans, and deftly rewound cassettes by manually whirling the sprockets with hexagonal Bic pens to conserve power.) The building itself was testimony to this kind of make-do endurance. We'd see in a place like Svirstroy an affront to newness, which in America is the

path to the future, and our sensibility might prove problematic, on the level of some aesthetic or metaphoric
blockage, in kicking off a project like an orphanage. We'd
wonder how you could hope to offer children a future in a
building so evidently scarred by the past.

The very best night I spent at the orphanage was with a
young woman named Yana. She was sixteen, and lived
with four other girls, dorm-style, in a room she'd occupied
for the past nine years. You could feel the resonance her
long tenure brought to the space. She'd obviously lavished
love on it, which in turn probably set the tone for the other
girls. The economy of love in the orphanage seemed to
work that way; it was passed quite efficiently from one kid
to the next. Love spread horizontally, across the broad,
extended present of the orphanage; it wasn't invested in a
future or sequestered in a solitary, longed-for past. The
beds were neatly, uniformly made, with pleasant colorful
quilts and matching pillowcases, and Yana had strung a
philodendron on monofilament so that, trained, its
healthy green cordate leaves circled the room airily overhead, like a string of unripe hearts. On the walls were glitzy
pictures of Britney Spears, Christina Aguilera, etc.; at one
point Yana got up, peeled back the corner of a poster, and
showed the cracked plaster beneath; she'd put the pictures
there to cover what she called "the bad places." She was a

little shy about it, shy as if the damaged plaster reflected on her personally, but she also seemed proud of the improvements she'd made. She had rodents, like the boys, but these were cute, cuddly mice, a boy and a girl, and she kept them in a large jar of soft, fine wood shavings and, with no divider, planned to share the eventual offspring with other kids in the orphanage.

Yana had been at Svirstroy for eleven years. She said she had no idea where her mother and father were, but presumably they were somewhere, alive; an uncle, alcoholic, last paid her a visit in 1995.

She asked if I'd like to see her photo album, and when I said I would the room suddenly got very quiet. And then her shier roommates, encouraged, brought out their albums. It's hard to imagine or adequately describe what an album of photographs might mean to an orphaned girl of sixteen. One thing that was immediately apparent was that Yana herself did not own a camera. The pictures in her possession were taken by others, by visiting Americans, by one or two kids who'd been adopted and then sent back snapshots of themselves in Disneyland, by representatives of the various charitable organizations that come through a couple times a year. In other words, they were copies of photographs taken, most centrally, as an event in someone else's life. Yana herself was a touristic stop in somebody's trip to Russia. In every single shot she was posed; there were no candid moments, no moments outside the fragilely constructed instant. Naturally, the pictures didn't serve a nostalgic function. They hardly offered a chronology, capturing instead the present tense of life at Svirstroy. The scenery surrounding Yana never changed radically; the orphanage was her constant backdrop. Judging by the album alone, Yana was never a baby, she was never a toddler taking a first step, she was never a communicant in white lace walking up the aisle at church, she'd never had a birthday or ridden a bike, etc., etc. In a way, family photographs are a record of the parents' watchful eyes, a chart of the unfolding future they've planned and invested in, but a sense of that forward-looking scrutiny was entirely absent in her album. These photographs were taken by strangers, and some of that exchange, the character of it, remained in every picture, in the posed quality, the drifting gaze, the blank or baffled or forced expression. In a regular family album, the kids grow, their bodies change, and that's largely what's being documented; and half the time the true subject is in the background, it's about a day at the beach, it's about the snow in the mountains, it's about the garden in back of grandma's house—it's about the children as they exist in the world. But in Yana's album there was no such verification. She existed, solely, at the orphanage.

When I asked the kids if they were happy, none of them could really answer; the question, I gathered, was puzzling.

"Happiness is a big word," Tonia told me, after a long, stalled silence. Then, through the translator of course, she said she was happiest when there was understanding, when "things go good for others," when people love each other. I realized then that I was asking a typically American question about the state or sovereignty of the self. It was a question that assumed a primary and absolute right to an interior self, and she, like so many of the kids, looked instead to the outer world, the world of contact, of presence. Eventually, she did say one of her best memories was when the other kids surprised her with a gift and a cake and lemonade at a birthday party she wasn't expecting. What seemed to move Tonia was that they'd "prepared ahead," that she'd been held in mind by others, remembered for a duration, and given a passing sense of what a future, filled with loving concern, might feel like. And that's the way it was at Svirstroy. None of the kids expressed a sense of being rooked out of an imagined rightful life, and if perhaps, darkly, they'd developed minds and equipped their souls with buffers so pain was not cumulative and the present tense of experience neither stemmed from the past nor was predicated on a future, so be it. They were home.

One day I was led through the woods by ten or so kids until we came to a spring that emerged from the base of a hummock marked by a large Russian Orthodox cross. A small wooden platform had been placed beside the spring, to stand on as you fetched water; next to it was a forked

stick, like a coat rack, dangling with drinking cups someone had made by cutting plastic bottles in half. We all
drank, and the water was cool and clean, it felt like water
should feel, holy, a moment where time stops, and the
quenching of thirst, on that day as on any really good day
in your life, was as much a matter of communion as breaking bread or sharing wine. In some simple way this was the
site of a special meaning, and the kids had led me, like an
acolyte, to a place where I could drink and refresh myself
in a communal mystery. Svirstroy was a place where love
circulated, and somehow what's good there was registering
in me. I was feeling it. I'm sure I was. These children never
showed self-pity, and if anything they'd taken the hollow
where that emotion normally settles and filled it with each
other. In fairy tales every juncture along the trail, no matter how dark or forbidding, is met with a yes, and that's
how they unfold and why, deep down, they soothe our
fears. Here, inside the shared present, was the happiness
Tonia was talking about.

It's natural enough to hope tomorrow will cure today, and
the core of the problem, of futures that recoup current dif-
ficulties, cropped up again when the translator brought to
my attention the business of money: his $200, the orphan-
age's $150, the driver's $300, the hotel's $200, none of
which I had. I was dead broke. I'd traveled halfway around

the world with a dollar in my left pocket that was more talisman or trinket than anything else. I'd been boldly approached by a lovely Russian hooker in the lobby of the Moscow Hotel, a beautiful blonde with Heidi braids and endearing broken English and a Russian Novel name, Katarina, all very tempting, but that transaction, like everything else, was beyond my means. She refused to believe I was broke. We argued about it! She wanted to know how much money I made "every month in America." I felt like we were trying to negotiate a swap of cultural clichés. I was too embarrassed to tell her that basically my mother and sister and brother-in-law had been supporting me until my new mood stabilizers kicked in and I could once again think clearly about my life, i.e., get out of bed in the morning. For the kids at Svirstroy, the circulation of money, Russian or otherwise, was never an issue. Most of the boys beyond the age of ten smoke, and cigarettes, for them, act as a kind of coin, a wealth to be acquired and traded and shared. The absence of "real" money, fiat money, is essentially the absence of a future. Not that the boys lack one—rather, possible futures never enter into their calculations; a cigarette equals pleasure, not the hoarding of deferred possibilities. In America, the sight of little boys with cigarettes would be shocking, but I have to say these guys were kind of cute, in a Little Rascally way, puffing smokes in their sloppy orphan clothes.

The other currency we traded in was words. None of the kids spoke English, although one boy I really liked a lot, Sasha, would say, "Good morning. I'm glad to see you." And other kids liked floating the few words they knew my way. They traded these words like chits in a game about relationships: Limp Bizkit, hip-hop, Linkin Park, etc. Language probably always has this adhesive aspect, but it's more noticeable when you struggle for words, when you constantly skirt the edges of failure. When I was on my own, alone with the kids, they either shouted in Russian, as if I were merely dense, or worked with gestures, as though playing charades. The translator was meant to bridge the gap, and he was excellent, keeping the conversation alive to the point that, after a few days, the kids began to realize that I could, on occasion, be pretty funny, and I, in turn, was just beginning to recognize the soulful texture, the nap of personality, in some of the boys and girls I spent the most time with. On the upside, perhaps, our lack of shared language had a filtering effect—rather like a lack of money—giving the past a shallowness, the future a vagueness, and keeping us in an essential present. Paradoxically, translation and the stripping of tenses forced us to live together in a physical, shared world. We enjoyed the fresh air, the river, the smell of pine trees. We played games that didn't require talk, and we walked the trails and pathways, letting those old sentences in the forests surrounding Svirstroy speak. Still, working through a translator was hard. Everything came close to a gloss or a paraphrase, losing some degree of nuance, so that it was very difficult to know who was quick-witted or sullen or sensitive, which kids were bright and which were slow. There were questions I didn't ask, particularities and depths I avoided. This failure on the level of fine distinction tends to make you see the kids as a conglomerate, which points the way toward pity, opening you up to a vague and general sadness at exactly the moment when, because you'll never have to do anything particular, it's safe.

One little thing I saw over and over again filled me with a low-grade despair and a lingering, elusive sadness I could never quite identify. Even now I can only approach it roundaboutly.

A lot of things the kids were into had a definite prison character. I don't mean the kids were criminal or delinquent, not by a long shot, but there was a sense of damaged or boxed-up futurity, similar in feature, though less extreme, to convicts. A book of matches had a fairly high valuation, as did cigarettes, stickers, and hair clips, which was more the sign of an underlying scarcity and an uncertain future than a reflection of real cost. These things were squeezed for every remaining ounce of meaning. Some of the boys held onto dead batteries, for instance, collecting them for their trinket value long after they'd lost their utility. Hair clips and cigarettes are known as commodity money, money with intrinsic value, which is close kin to barter and, at this point, at least in modern societies, a very distant relation to fiat money, which has no intrinsic value. The few times I saw the kids with cash, the bills actually looked more like a strange text than a token of value. If fiat money speaks to the future or, through debt, keeps up a conversation with the past, then barter addresses the present— it's about now. Being broke can make for a kind of immediacy, and so can bartering, if being exposed to vicissitudes, quite nakedly, without defense, is the measure; whereas fiat money and fluid markets free us up from time and space, the local insults of the seasons, the impoverishment of the soil beneath our feet, etc. But when the future suffers a disturbance, as it does for an orphaned child or prisoner, or as it often does in war, money either tends toward barter or finds more fluidity by going underground. About Warsaw during World War II, Czeslaw Milosz says: "Life, as for primitive man, once more depended on the seasons of the year. Autumn was the hardest because potatoes and coal had to be gotten for the long, hopeless winter."

The curious tension here is that children are the future, and the ruptured promise a place like Svirstroy tries to repair is vast. The future requires kids; without them, there's eventually no tomorrow. In time, of course, everybody runs out of tomorrows. The one thing you can say about the future, Joseph Brodsky has written, is that it won't include you. That's true, and yet the dyad of money and children plots you way out there in that world of tomorrows you don't get. Your dream, then, is of a noth- ingness where an investment of love lives on. You believe in a time that's not your own. The main problem with barter is the need for a coincidence of wants: you have to want what the other person's got, and vice versa. And you have to arrive at a specific place in the universe on time. Most basically we no longer barter much because we don't want to entrust our dinner to the cosmos, which is likely empty. And here's the thing that was so hard for me to feel precisely: over and over, what I saw at Svirstroy were these little hands passing things, bottle caps and cigarettes, a cookie, a twig or leaf, small frequent exchanges where skin contacted skin, just briefly, but perfectly timed, now. In the enormity of their dislocation, the kids arrived for each other, always. They were there, they were present, and bar- tering was the deal that confirmed it. It made me sad, these transactions, these little dirty hands reaching and finding, this coincidence of wants, taking place inside a huge broken promise. Born into a world where their wants went unmet, where their time was taken away, they found reassuring coincidence in bartering. In those little moments I felt like I was seeing the kids isolated—lovingly so—in currents that were crushing them.

———

But let's say, since it's natural enough, that tomorrow really is a remedy for today. Back in St. Petersburg there was still the heavily pending matter of money. The translator came to the Moscow Hotel on Saturday, ostensibly to arrange for a transfer of funds and then take me to a public market, where I hoped to pick up a few souvenirs. Plus, I wanted to return his abundant kindness by treating him to a nice dinner. The good people at *Nest* had wired cash, and I was relieved, even feeling magnanimous, like a regular, upright, solvent citizen. The translator handed me a receipt, and I noticed all the agreed-upon prices had been jacked up by thirty dollars, like a customs or tariff on my confusion. He called the bank but the phone just rang and rang. Then he said we'd take a cab to the bank, as if that were a reasonable assumption to draw from an unanswered phone. Myself, I pictured an empty, dark room, but the translator must have imagined something else; what, I don't know. We caught a jitney cab, just some beat guy driving around in a Lada, and for a hundred rubles, roughly three dollars, he drove us way the hell out past a ghetto of gray Soviet housing, into a flat wasteland reclaimed from swamp sometime in the eighteenth century. Three hundred years later the swamp seemed to be rising, phoenixlike, in the form of pale white dust. The roads were fucked—islands of level pavement surrounded by deep holes. All our business—cab fare, directions, destination— was being conducted in Russian, of course, so when we arrived at a sprawling compound fenced and topped with razor wire, the mystery had a gentle logic that even the uniformed guards, with machine guns slung over their shoulders, couldn't dispel, not entirely. The Russians had seemed weird about money and market efficiency, and perhaps guys with guns made more sense in the former Republic than a row of tellers. The translator looked at the place and said, "Strange."

We finally found the building, found the room number, and knocked on the door, even though it was slightly ajar in a very unbanklike manner. There was no one inside. The room didn't even remotely resemble a bank, although perhaps interior space needs a translator as much as language does. The translator talked at length with a woman across the hall, who'd been sitting, alone, in a nearly identical room, reading a paperback novel, and who insisted there was no bank in the compound. We quickly flagged down another crappy Lada and rode a completely different way back to the Moscow Hotel and made more phone calls in pursuit of the money. It all felt like a shell game and, anyway, I wanted to hurry out and buy a chess set for my niece and maybe visit Anna Akhmatova's last residence, now a museum. I was hoping to hang out at Dostoevsky's tomb too, especially since old Fyodor, beset by gambling debts most of his life, was starting to seem like the patron saint of my trip. However, it seemed unlikely that the translator, disappointed about the money, was going to take me to any markets or show me the way to some old poet's house, and ultimately he just left me on my own and said good-bye. He'd lost his interest in me. Maybe he was broke too.

Back at the orphanage, a day earlier, one of the kids, Ruslan, had asked me a riddle. There's a donkey, he said, trapped on an island in the middle of the ocean. A volcano is erupting on the island and rivers of hot lava are flowing toward the donkey. In addition, all around the small island is a ring of fire. What, Ruslan wanted to know, would you do? I thought about it, came up blank, and said I didn't know. And Ruslan, with a smile, said: the donkey didn't know either.

Documents

Poem by Father (1972)

One Sunday morning when I was a boy, my father came out of his office and handed me a poem. It was about a honeybee counseling a flea to flee a doggy and see the sea. The barbiturates my father took to regulate his emotions made him insomniac, and I understood that he'd been awake most of the night, laboring over these lines, listing all the words he could think of ending in a long "e." This meant using many adverbs and the elevated "thee" as a form of address. My father was a professor of finance who wrote fairly dry textbooks, where the prose marched in soldierly fashion across the page, broken by intricate formulas calculating risk and return, and this poem was a somewhat frilly production for him. The poem was an allegory about his desire to leave our family. Like a lot of people my father felt a poem was a bunch of words with a tricky meaning deeply buried away, like treasure, below a surface of rhyming sounds. I was twelve years old, and I understood the sense of the poem instantly, but the strange mixture of childish diction and obvious content silenced me. I was ashamed. That Sunday morning, I was sitting on the living room floor, on a tundra of white carpet my father considered elegant. The drapes were closed, because he worried that sun would fade the fabric on the furniture, but a bright bar of light cut through a gap in the curtains, and that's where I sat, since it was warm there, in a house where we were otherwise forbidden to adjust the thermostat above sixty-two degrees.

Letter from younger brother (1997)

Not long ago, I was in Seattle, sitting in a café downtown. It was raining. I'd been there for some time before I realized that someone was staring at me through the window. I turned around and saw worn tennis shoes and dirty gray sweats. The man outside the window was my brother Mike. My father had three sons. I'm the eldest; Danny, the youngest, killed himself sixteen years ago.

In addition to the tennis shoes and sweats, Mike was wearing a white T-shirt that hung to his knees and a black leather jacket he'd bought with VA money at a thrift store. His thinning hair was soaked, and his face had the pallor of warm cheese. In a plastic sack he carried a carton of cigarettes he'd bought at the Navy PX. He's schizophrenic and on some level I'm always aware that he's a stranger. I went outside and we talked and, in talking, we were brothers again. He did not look good; he was shivering. He was several miles from his halfway house, but when I offered to give him a ride he said, quite happily, that he preferred to walk. He started up the hill, limping a little from a pelvic injury he received, years ago, when he tried to kill himself by jumping off the Aurora Bridge in Seattle. Very soon he was gone.

Only a few years ago, Mike had been doing much better, and he wrote letters regularly, often two or three a month. Here is one:

Dear Char,

Mike here, who is there? I am fine as a blade of grass. How about you?

As I was leaving church the other day there was an opportunity to be part of a poor person's Kriss Kringle. I decided to buy an AIDS patient some high-quality gloves. The situation reminded me of Danny—I don't know why. The gift will be given to him although I believe I will never actually see the recipient. I will give him a card that says, "To a friend I don't know."

I don't think of Danny a lot. I don't feel pain about his death a lot either. Jesus has stepped into his boots and has replaced him. It caused me to heal and be born again. It is really quite beautiful. My heart is still with that kid like you cannot believe—or I suppose you could. Love can play a trick on you. It can cause you pain like you were suffering in hell but it is still love and still beautiful like heaven and the heaven and the hell of it are woven into one fabric, which is love. It's a mindblower to think like that but that is what Danny has done to me.

Call or write please.

I don't own a cat or dog—but I do the same by looking at squirrels and crows. I plan to buy some peanuts to feed the squirrels and bread for the birds. It is so much cheaper and I enjoy it the same as having my own animal.

When I pray I can see my life flash before my eyes. It is very beautiful. My life flashes before my eyes about twenty times a year. Other stuff like that happens to me also.

I've been through so much since becoming mentally ill—most of it, believe it or not, was good. Because of that I became sort of an indestructible man.

Love, Mike

Letter from youngest brother (November 26, 1986)
My brother Danny wrote his suicide note in my bedroom, and then, after a caesura that I know exists because he had to put down the pen in order to pick up the gun, he shot himself. For some reason, I've always been concerned about the length of the lapse, whether he reread what he'd

written or stared dumbly at his signature, his name the final piece in a puzzling life he was about to end, before he pressed the gun to his head and pulled the trigger. Most suicides go about the last phase of their business in silence and don't leave notes. Death itself is the summary statement, and they step into its embrace hours or days before the barrel is finally raised to the roof of the mouth or the fingertips last feel the rough metal of the bridge rail. They are dead and then they die. But Danny wrote a note, or not so much a note as an essay, a long document full of self-hatred and sorrow, love and despair, and now I'm glad that I have it, because, this way, we're still engaged in a dialogue. His words are there and so is his hand, a hand I'd held, but, more important, one that left words, like an artifact, that are as real and physical to me as the boy who, at twenty-one, in a November long ago, wrote them.

I read the pages he wrote two or three times a month, often enough so that the words ring like the lines of poems I know well. All the struggle is still there in the headlong sentences that tumble toward his signature, in the misspelled words and syntactical errors, in the self-conscious language of a boy starved for love and trying, instead, to live a moment more off pride. The note has the back-and-forth of a debate, of words equally weighed and in balance, of a slightly agonized civility. He says, "I stopped making dreams." He says, "I don't know why I am doing this. I don't want to. I have dreams." He says that there is no God and that God is looking over his shoulder as he writes, making editorial remarks. He says, "I am glorifying myself now. I am afraid to stop writing though. I want to keep talking." He says, "I don't know what to say except I am sorry and I love. I love the whole family quite a bit and the terrible—" He clearly wants to find a way back, but he can't. He asks that we keep "the way" he died a secret and, as though he were done, signs his name. But on the next page, the last, he again asks that we keep "the way" he died secret, and again he signs his name. Much of the note is printed and those letters stand upright, but in the end Danny slips permanently into a sloping cursive as despair and self-hatred accelerate beyond return, as if he were being pulled down by the dark undercurrent of his life, his last words looping quickly across the page, continuous as breath.

Letter from eldest brother (2001)

Two years ago, I moved to Philipsburg, Montana. In the fall, I went for walks and brought home bones. The best bones weren't on trails—deer and moose don't die conveniently—and soon I was wandering so far into the woods that I needed a map and compass to find my way home. When winter came and snow blew into the mountains, burying the bones, I continued to spend my days and often my nights in the woods. I vaguely understood that I was doing this because I could no longer think; I found relief in walking up hills. When the night temperatures dropped below zero, I felt visited by necessity, a baseline purpose, and I walked for miles, my only objective to remain upright, keep moving, preserve warmth. When I was lost, I told myself stories, recounting my survival, implying that I would live and be able to look back at it all. At some point, I realized that I was telling my father these stories.

I decided that I would try corresponding with him. I had built a lean-to at seven thousand feet, and I routinely slept there. In the morning, I warmed myself by a fire and then walked home and began writing. I worked for days, even weeks, on the letters. The last time I'd seen him he made a point of showing me the stains in his bed, on the sheets. He pulled away the blankets, revealing bright yellow splotches of mustard, red patches of spaghetti sauce, something urinous that had spilled from a carton of take-out Chinese. I'm not sure what he meant to show me, and I'm not sure what saddened me more, this man eating alone in bed, who could not clean up after himself, or this man who needed to share with his son a grotesque failure. My father and I had survived the same wounds. His lost sons were my brothers. I believed we might have something to talk about. I was drawn to the antique idea of a correspondence because it seemed restrained and formal, even ritualized. In Philipsburg, there is no home delivery, and people go to town to pick up mail. I always walked to the post office with my dog, and even that little effort, the mile of dirt road, blowing with dust or running with mud or silent under new snow, made the mail that much more meaningful.

I delayed sending my first letter for several months. My father replied with a long, bulleted outline. I read it, bullet by bullet, feeling disoriented, despite the orderly indents and the nesting of what, in outlines, are called "children." After four or five readings I was able to breathe normally. I reread his outline until I lost its meaning, then got out my colored pens and began highlighting. The bullets and dashes and indentations were like the sleeves and straps and buckles of a straitjacket. I've often thought that the unit of measure that best suits prose is the human breath, but there was no air in my father's sentences; he seemed to be suffocating inside them.

I had made an effort to discuss the events of our past, but he regarded this as a trespass. "When did God empower you," he asked me, "with such omniscient abilities?" His position was truth; mine was not. My letter, he wrote, "is incorrect throughout, is a fictional (Having no foundation in fact, OED) version of reality (Reality: The quality of being real or having an actual existence, OED)." He was defensive, which I should have anticipated: "After nine years of sixty-hour weeks of intensive research, not reading and study, but research, I know I was a terrific dad and terrific husband."

I wrote more letters. His replies were long—seven, eight, nine pages. There were words he couldn't get past. He became obsessed with "boundaries." Boundaries were bad. "Those who set them up," he wrote, "protect the dysfunctionality they see in themselves and seek to foist that malady on others through their boundaries." Boundaries, he wrote, "are the antithesis of meaningful honest relations." Boundaries have no place between a father and his children. He insisted the proper word was "relation." "Relation is a mathematical notion which means one-to-one correspondence."

Another time, it was the word "gag." He had used the word, saying that I was prevented from speaking honestly; I objected; he objected to my objection: "Emphasis on the word, gag, denies the act!!! The gag is the aggressive act. The word gag fits, is proportional to, the act. The gag is the loaded act; the word gag fits the denigrative power of the act. The act, not the word, is aggressive and odious. Place the focus where it belongs, properly, on the aggressive and repugnant act, and not on the word."

Some nights, I dug into the lee of a snowdrift and hollowed a shelter for myself. Snow contains air and insulates, holding the body's warmth so that, at a certain point, the temperature remains constant, blood and ice in equilibrium. In deep snow, I dragged supplies with a pulk I'd made from a child's sled and plastic conduit. I was afraid of avalanches and checked a slope meter before traversing open, treeless hillsides. What I feared was suffocation, particularly the inability to make my chest expand. I really knew nothing about winter, nothing about surviving the season beyond the blunt lesson in fatality I'd learned from picking up bones. Sometimes I slept in the open mouths of mine shafts, their crumbled headframes like broken teeth, where twice I found clusters of bats, hanging by their feet, their wings folded in, like the strange fruits of darkness itself.

I wrote, asking him about our home movies. For years I'd kept alive the fantasy that he burned the movies, only because I was haunted by the image of them orphaned in a Salvation Army thrift shop, reels and reels of birthdays, Christmases, and Easters, all reduced to an ironic treasure for strangers. In the past, I had wanted to believe my father was a liar rather than a man who could destroy something so valuable to his children. The movies were old Super-8s, poorly lit and without sound, but the only place left where I could see my brother's face.

I wrote, "You intentionally destroyed something inside your children, a place of warmth and fondness, a cherished dream, a continuity that connects us in time to our history and across space to one another."

Degrees of Gray in Philipsburg

Degrees of Gray in Philipsburg

Richard Hugo

You might come here Sunday on a whim.
Say your life broke down. The last good kiss
you had was years ago. You walk these streets
laid out by the insane, past hotels
that didn't last, bars that did, the tortured try
of local drivers to accelerate their lives.
Only churches are kept up. The jail
turned 70 this year. The only prisoner
is always in, not knowing what he's done.

The principal supporting business now
is rage. Hatred of the various grays
the mountain sends, hatred of the mill,
The Silver Bill repeal, the best liked girls
who leave each year for Butte. One good
restaurant and bars can't wipe the boredom out.
The 1907 boom, eight going silver mines,
a dance floor built on springs—
all memory resolves itself in gaze,
in panoramic green you know the cattle eat
or two stacks high above the town,
two dead kilns, the huge mill in collapse
for fifty years that won't fall finally down.

Isn't this your life? That ancient kiss
still burning out your eyes? Isn't this defeat
so accurate, the church bell simply seems
a pure announcement: ring and no one comes?
Don't empty houses ring? Are magnesium
and scorn sufficient to support a town,
not just Philipsburg, but towns
of towering blondes, good jazz and booze
the world will never let you have
until the town you came from dies inside?

Say no to yourself. The old man, twenty
when the jail was built, still laughs
although his lips collapse. Someday soon,
he says, I'll go to sleep and not wake up.
You tell him no. You're talking to yourself.
The car that brought you here still runs.
The money you buy lunch with,
no matter where it's mined, is silver
and the girl who serves your food
is slender and her red hair lights the wall.

His response was icy: "Of what sense of warmth and fondness are you speaking? It is an interesting sentiment, laced with some romanticism, but devoid of reality." And he wanted to know, "What did I destroy in you that was not already destroyed?"

In my father's last letter, the grammar carries the summary tone of a narrative closing down. It is framed by the forms of family affection. He opens with "Dear Char" and parts with "Love," followed by his signature. In between, the language suggests closure, termination. My previous letter, he says, continued an "unacceptable tenor and dead-end focus." It smacked of "recidivism"; it followed a "desolate and vacuous path." None of my letters "added a repairment." "So be it," he says.

I sometimes wonder if by "repairment" he meant "repayment," and I always pause at the caesura created by the simple sentence, "So be it," which Catholic kids were once taught is the meaning of "Amen." Was this the phrase that ran through my brother's mind as he paused between his two signatures? *So be it:* with these, my father's last words, I know I will never hear from him again. But I save his letters, as I save Danny's, as I save Mike's, neatly bound and held between the Army-surplus boots that my brother died in, and which I keep, filled with rocks, on my desk.

The streets of Philipsburg do indeed seem laid out by the insane. Beyond West Broadway pavement gives out, and from then on the roads and streets are a seasonal affair, running with mud or bleached by dust or silent under new snow. Many of the streets that cut through town barely qualify as such; they are paths beaten in the grass, two tracks where trucks lurch over rocks with a clatter of bad linkage, roads of gravel or red cinder that skirt empty pastures and a few last houses until they head, somewhat pointlessly now, into the hills and mountains where men once worked. One can imagine many things about these evocative streets, and in some ways that's all that remains, imagination haunting a town where even history, usually the last to leave, has given up and gone away. One can imagine, for instance, that the roads are the ripped seams of a civilization, rents in the fabric that have led to a general unraveling, to the vacant storefronts and faded signs and a rusting school bus, still yellow, inexplicably parked in front of a hotel whose last guest signed his name to the register, one vanished afternoon, years ago. Perhaps the bus died there, the children walked to school that morning, and it was convenient and reasonable, since weeds had already grown up around the red brick steps and the windows were gone and the hotel, it was agreed, by some vague assent, was never coming back, to leave the bus where it was, like the carcass of a whale washed to shore. Time would take care of it, as it had the hotel. Now the bus has no windows, and who knows what became of the children. You don't see many of them on the streets of Philipsburg.

One can imagine the roads—somehow the word "streets" implies too much, is too elaborate—as the relics of haste and ambition, of a boom in silver that lasted a few short years, until the Repeal—and that word, *repeal*, seems fitting for a town whose future was never in its own hands—disrupted the hurried energy, and in fact crimped the flow of time generally. Houses had been flung up on the hillsides, and there was some need to connect them, but the original roads were probably platted by the tramping of tired men. That weariness, that exhaustion, is inscribed in the roads to this day. Things of course changed, but in some ways time reversed direction and began running backwards, seeking the past as water does low level. But nostalgia, where loss finds rest, hasn't really taken root.

Philipsburg's rival from the boom era, Granite, several miles back in the woods, higher and colder and more remote, is a ghost town now, the last resident, holding out as he worked a small claim, having died seventy years ago. You can walk those streets and still find the infirmary and the bank vault and the music hall and, pointedly, down a gully, the obligatory red light district that seems always to follow wherever the work men do is an insult to their bodies. Presently someone is trying to rebuild the town, hoping to attract tourists, and on most Sundays in the summer, a few desultory visitors wander with a photocopied map through stands of stunted pine, looking, somewhat puzzled, at walls of leaning brick or the fairly intact stone house of the superintendent. Some of the shacks where miners lived still have their sad beds shoved into a corner, although those shacks are so small they seem to be made up solely of corners. A black stove, a chair by the window, and the space is filled. The size of these clapboard shanties doesn't suggest children, and it's as if the future, even from the beginning, was something you would have to establish in another town. The past was Granite's destiny from day one, and when the mines shut down for good, what was left of that past was packed up and moved in carts three miles down the mountain, settling in Philipsburg.

————

Entitling a poem or story or essay is harder than naming a child. The privilege of place is almost like a law of primogeniture, with the title inheriting the entire work, and along with that legacy comes the burden, the implied promise, of carrying the weight of the piece to the end. You want to avoid the didactic as well as a too vaguely allusive reference that will read portentously. Joyce named things well—"The Dead," *A Portrait of the Artist as a Young Man, Ulysses*—suggesting by example that simplicity and a certain cool aim at the center of a work is the way to go. Hugo's title goes that way, and yet I've always liked it, in part, because shadings of gray refer to weather, and weather is only mentioned once, obliquely, in a line of the poem where, even then, the accent falls on another word. This seems characteristic of a poet who is both blunt and self-effacing: the poem avoids wallowing in its most obvious mood. But while we're promised degrees of gray, like a chromatic study in painting, we descend through the poem, down through the broken self and ruined history and a stanza of questions with no satisfying answers, until we arrive at the final lines, in which, suddenly, a slender girl's red hair lights the wall. To a point, in other words, where the color red is the hero of the poem. Hugo is an honest writer, and his title is honest, I believe, but the light and youth and especially the vivid red, discovered down at the bottom of everything, is the one note in the poem that has always put me in a questioning, objecting state of mind. I've always felt—just vaguely, like a hitch in my reading—that Hugo pulled the red out of his hat.

After the onslaught of loss, both personal and historical, do we really believe a good lunch and an aesthetic perception settles the matter? Does red (and, by inference, poetry) save? Quite possibly poetry salvages nothing except language itself, and even that project of reclamation is up against poor odds. Poetry is not a social program and it's not easily accessible to everyone, despite its ancient mnemonic role and the currency of certain opinions by primitivists of the New Age. Nor is poetry liturgical, composed of sacramental language and containing a central mystery that can be approached, shared, and repeated, then made portable and evangelized and kept alive through ritual until its power rivals governments. The Pauline hopes of poetry recur now and then—in Shelley or Brodsky, for instance, or Edward Hirsch—but they don't result in many converts. Reading poems remains a cult practice of the few, and it's hard to imagine an art form further in temper from the reality of Philipsburg. Hugo's red might be epiphanic and passing, one of those visions we expect a poet to access, an insight confirming our solitude rather than rescuing us from it, but if this is so, does he really touch the ruin so richly itemized in the rest of the poem? Hugo's no aesthete, and he means for this red to be a real outcome, an inevitable result of looking directly at the degrees of gray. Because he's a poet, we have to take him at his word. Hugo says there's salvation in poetry, a saving, moreover, discovered at the bottom of ruin, and he's also suggesting, I think, that you must fall to find it.

I don't want to bog down in the exegetical rigging of real criticism, the cumbersome quoting, the whole vast tackle of arcane and specialized language that takes poetry further toward silence. Hugo's poem doesn't require it. It's written in free verse, sprung from the inner clock that keeps time in metrical poetry, and so the lines read like regular sentences, denser but not all that different from the ones in a daily newspaper. The poem's not fragile. You can beat on it. It's got good traction. Paraphrased, its four stanzas go like this:

1. You're fucked.
2. We're all fucked.
3. Why?
4. Let's eat lunch.

It isn't easy to say your life broke down. It isn't easy to say in conversation and expect anyone to listen, and it's desperately hard to say in poetry or prose and expect anyone to read. From my own experience I know the result, most of the time, is laughable. On a personal level, the problem seems to be that we know these things happen, but we don't ultimately know why they do, and anyone who steps forward too ready with phrases from pop psychology or offering details from personal history is either missing the deeper point or airing gripes. The problem for the poet is one of expression; nothing is quite so false, in writing, as the heartfelt confession. Irony in its least waggish form, scrubbed of cynicism, is necessary—a certain cool, a distance, the slight masking that occurs whenever the writer separates from his subject. Hugo's solution is to go for blunt, and most of this poem trades in symbols that batter the obvious, from broken-down cars to crazy streets to churches and jails and a prisoner, not knowing what he's done, who stands in for the state of the soul. The symbolism here is too much in the public domain, too shared for this to be a private excursion. Even if you wanted to, you couldn't wring a proprietary solitude from it. When Hugo says your life broke down, that's either metonymy or synecdoche, but we get the point, that its absent term is a car, and we accept it because of the banged-up humor and his refusal to be pretty about it. The directness is disarming, and it serves the subject—even our most durable, readily available solutions have failed. These symbols create a loneliness and isolation because their communal function has failed, but we still recognize their ghostly hopes as our own. In a single stanza Hugo sweeps up the whole of Western civilization. There are plenty of mouths but the kiss that really eludes us is the good one—*failed love.* The streets are nuts, they either don't go anywhere or, if they do, all the destinations are dead ends—*failed thought*. Churches are kept up, but a church qua building is only a maintenance problem, no longer in the business of salvation—*failed spirit*. The hotels haven't lasted, and the jail's already lived out its Biblical allotment of years—*failed alibi, law*. You're a wreck, but you've come to a place that's an even worse mess—*failed individual, society*.

The auxiliary verb "might" subtly, brilliantly alters the universe, so that the "you" is not the poet addressing himself, or not strictly. If, instead, Hugo writes: You *came* here Sunday . . . then we're into confining facts, confessional accounts, moving a step away from the poem as written, with its broad, inclusive "you," toward the self as a dead end, seeking private salvations. The "you" would then become the poet or a character standing in for the poet, and in any case, whatever hope or possibility the poem holds would be bracketed by the past tense, framed inside personal history, absorbed into a character whose formation was completed some time ago—into a world, in other words, that occurred, once and for all, prior to the poem. The perfect past would isolate the poet from his poem, quarantining the ruin to a time and place that's already been safely escaped; the poem would be the artifact left behind by an experience, losing an element of risk. Using the auxiliary *might* shifts the tone. We enter the poem through supposition, and are given, like an allowance, a small sum of uncertainty, to spend wisely or foolishly. By rescuing the first line from a finished past tense, *might* hints at a future, particularly in the sense that anything unknown belongs to an expectant time. It plants a seed of probability or possibility, even advisability. The word's brassy note rings like a harmonic, its long vowel sound finally flicking light against the wall, but how do we get there?

In this first stanza, the lines are typically short and flat, somewhat immobile, and the one line that departs from the pattern, the longest and most fluent, is about movement, particularly walking and acceleration. It's as if the poem panics inside its contracted space. Pathetically, it wants to go somewhere. The syntax is an echo of the sense, and there's fear and alarm in the sentence, a struggle between understanding and action, capturing a moment of awareness and the ensuing paralysis, when flight is the right impulse but the urge has atrophied and there really isn't anywhere to go. Each hurried clause is like a frightened, fading footstep. And then the urge dies, the brief flight stops, and the sentences, abrupt as walls, return to their immobility. The prisoner is always in—a curious phrase, in that he doesn't seem to be held against his will. He doesn't need to be. Awareness is gone, and with it, freedom. His imprisonment is a condition. He's bound to a cell by "not knowing," which isn't a defect of mind, but of comprehension, one we all share regardless of native gifts. That the prisoner lacks understanding might serve as a legal argument for his innocence, but no ruling, for or against, will release him from history.

Philipsburg is located in the Flint Valley, a valley so open and wide all movement along the highway feels annulled, and on the morning of September 11 nothing here changed. The vast space seemed to cancel out even conversation, and there was no rush to talk about the attack in New York. I'm not now inclined to fill this silence with supposition, to hazard guesses about the particular quality of the quiet in Philipsburg, except to say I felt it myself. While I can imagine people in New York or Boston or Omaha stunned by fear and outrage, that wasn't my situation, and I remember standing outside that morning, looking across the valley where already, in the higher elevations, snow had fallen, and feeling nothing, not horror or disgust, not shock or anger. A branch snapped by a surprising June snow, a dry hummock up the hill where fox denned in winter, these things held my attention, standing out, strange and real, in the nearby world. It may be true that we are ultimately saved from total loss, as Czeslaw Milosz has written, because there's nothing to do but stare at the green leaf fluttering in the wind. Much of the news, as a form of expression, made little sense to me. People were saying our lives would never be the same again, a phrase turning naively around a moment that space, which is heartless, and nature, which is indifferent, would never share. Not even history agrees, and part of what made discussion so difficult was the intrusion of the historical into a romance, a confusion of genres we find particularly galling. Hawthorne called Romance "a legend prolonging itself," whose hostile enemy is contact with history. Without any real conscious intention, I would find myself seeking a sense of that contact, turning to the work of Milosz and Joseph Brodsky, writers who, knowing first-hand the horror of history, struggled between silence and noise to make their poems. But before that, days, a week after the attack, as voices emerged, as newscasters spoke, as opinions were aired, with noise becoming the norm, I found a photograph of a falling man that seemed to restore a necessary silence, and I pinned a copy to my wall. It seemed to me a place to begin, the only place.

Whereas prison, well, what is it? A shortage
of space compensated for by an excess of time.

—Joseph Brodsky

Brodsky's equation is just, I think, but you can tinker with
the terms and arrive at other prisons, other compensations.
This picture also brings us to a prison, one without a
shortage of space; in fact, there's a sudden, horrifying
excess, a terrible liberation, with time in short supply.

In this moment the falling man's time on earth is a
spatial concern, and he has more in common with a stapler
than he does with you or me. Natural laws explain why he's
dropping and a formula can easily calculate the rate of his
descent. A man of roughly that weight, from roughly that
height, in that specific gravity, arms and legs spread, reaches
a terminal velocity of 125 mph, beyond which there's
no further acceleration. Terminal velocity—of the man, a
stapler, a raindrop—is the square root of $[(2 \times W)/(Cd \times r \times A)]$.[1] That's the irresolvable contradiction in this picture,
a man subject to mechanistic forces, a life obedient to an
indifference—although obedient is a somewhat dead
metaphor here, since rebellion or refusal is impossible. One
might wonder if he jumped or not, a last act of volition,
a final insistence on self, but either way falling is the

1. Where W = weight, Cd = drag coefficient, r = density, and A = frontal area

consequence. In falling, he's lost connection, he's ripped free from every relation, to his love and work and family, to his own biography, to the choice he made that morning about what shirt to wear. The descent strips him of every cherished thing, even our regard, and one thinks of Auden's Old Masters who understood the position of human suffering, "how it takes place/While someone else is eating or opening a window or just walking dully along" and the amazing boy from Breughel, falling out of the sky, seen by a ship that had "somewhere to get to and sailed calmly on." The falling man is falling because that's what things do, and in some awful way it's not remarkable.

Just the same, there's an abstract purity to the picture, in the geometry of sky and building, that strangely suspends the man in a constructed space, entirely drained of time, so that one imagines him there forever. The composition is immaculate, even icily harmonious. In the picture's arrested moment you get a pure feel for the falling man's incomprehension, his emptiness, but in the days following the attack, obviously, this sensation would become intolerable to survivors, to the witnesses we were turned into, and the point of view would shift, the images would progress. Something was needed to distinguish the falling man from a fluttering scrap of paper, from the nothing of his silent descent. The pristine space began to blow with dust and fill with debris. Attention was focused on the broken hierarchy, the jumbled ruin. An accessible idea of heroism, Homeric but not tragic, occupied the human void, and suddenly firemen loomed up and moved across the foreground of the new images. "The savagery of the struggle for existence," Milosz has written, "is not averted by civilization," and now we knew this, possibly. But a hasty gloss of evolution from primitive to modern was improvised, phoenixlike, out of the ashes, and contra the terrorists, who seemed to have reduced a symbol of at least one kind of civilized aspiration to a barbaric rubble. Rebuilding began in a rudimental, dark, superstitious state where blind luck or chance either saved or did not save. Later, it turned out that God was with the people who survived and the people who perished were now with God, a tautological tidiness that always breaks my heart, tearing at an old longing for universal justice. Faces were shown, names mentioned, chronologies elaborated, stories told, helping to rehabilitate the present scene, applying a patch to the moral sense. An ideal *civitas* emerged, so that, looking into the shadowy precincts of Wall Street, where certainly some of the dead were embezzlers, no mention was made of precisely the sort of intrigants who would, later, populate stories about Enron. It's almost too obvious to state, but in a random sample of any three thousand people, some will be beating their children, others will be addicted to heroin, and others still will be caught in the midst of affairs that would, left to run their course, damage families and undo in some degree the social fabric. But this was a new polis—from which those folks were now symbolically banished. Sincerity worked like a conduit for connection. What might have been viewed as a great equalizer, falling on the just and unjust alike, visited on the rich and the poor, the fair and the homely, black and white, instead rose out of the wreckage with a perfectly familiar face, looking quite the same as life before. Hierarchy was restored, and hatred with it. Enemies were declared, war was in the offing, and now the falling man, not knowing what he'd done, was descending through—or perhaps into—the medium of history, which sits between all of us and oblivion.

There has been considerable reflection on the origins of the phenomenon known as individualism, or Byronic despair—the revolt of the individual who considers himself the center of all things, and their sole judge. No doubt, it was the contents of the imagination itself which forced this to happen, *as soon as hierarchical space began to somersault.* Anyone who looks into himself can reproduce the course of the crisis. The imagination will not tolerate dispersal and chaos, without maintaining one place to which all others are related, and, when confronted with an infinity of relationships, always relative only to each other, it seizes upon its sole support, the ego. So why not think of myself as an ideal incorporeal observer *suspended above the turning earth?*

—Czeslaw Milosz

Hatred organizes space—think of Dante's *Inferno*, the structure of which is partly animated by personal enmity—and in the gray waste of the Philipsburg in Hugo's poem, it's the principal supporting business. The contracted, hating ego restores hierarchy, creating an armature for the emotions, organizing a defense of the inner life while it's attacked from outside. But hate and rage are emotions we summon to survive a crisis, and the acute phase can't be sustained for long. The adrenal medulla can't hack it. The surge of epinephrine is meant to peak and subside and pass entirely with the passing of the injury or threat. Without relief the nerves blunt and even if the emergency remains, a numbing settles in obdurately; and that's the harmed, sinking, downward passage, from hatred to boredom, captured in the second stanza of the poem. Hugo moves in a quick line or two from rage and hatred to boredom, and I think he's right to push the association. Here, the hatred is against history, the mere unfolding of life, its indifferent or brutal or oblivious progress, against which the spiked rage can't strike out. It's a grievance against ghosts, a grievance against what's gone—or even, more accurately, against the sheer "going" of life everyone suffers. No wonder that in these ruined Western towns you so often find revivals along the lines of Hawthorne's legend prolonging itself, the sorry romance of the spurned, yearning to occupy the dramatic center once more by suspending time. The main drag in Philipsburg is either ruined or vacant or shabby or somewhat tartly gussied up, but these are all guises of the same settled arrangement, the same hierarchy. Hatred's destination is boredom, and boredom is perhaps a rebellion against time; it's the finished putting up a fight with the end. Boredom is, at any rate, a more habitable space, long-term, than history.

The British psychologist Adam Phillips calls boredom "that most absurd and paradoxical wish, the wish for a desire," and defined as such, boredom isn't fixed by distraction, by bars or restaurants, but by the arrival of a feeling of anticipation. I know for myself boredom involves a spatialization of time; the forwardness goes out of life, and I wait, and in waiting time becomes a place—not a particularly good one, but a place nonetheless, with the minutes and hours, the days and months piling up indifferently. For phenomenologists, this kind of repetition isn't a property of time but of space, and then it's more aptly called redundancy, when things exceed what's necessary. In boredom you take on some of the character of an object, becoming lifeless and inanimate, lacking flow, and the more the time sense is rendered into space, the more isolated you become—isolated by becoming extraneous. The spooky intimation behind boredom, the whispered secret of it, is death, a final draining of time, when at last all the living belong exclusively to space. In boredom, we become victims of a sameness within a hierarchy whose original principal of design was a now forgotten, vestigial loss of proportion—which is an aesthetic problem, the problem of arranging parts harmoniously within a whole.

> What is worse, time, always strongly spatial, has increased in spatiality; it has stretched infinitely back out behind us, infinitely forward into the future toward which our faces are turned. Today I cannot deny that in the background of all my thinking there is the image of the chain of development—of gaseous nebulae condensing into liquids and solid bodies, a molecule of life—begetting acid, species, civilizations succeeding each other in turn, segment added to segment, on a scale which reduces me to a particle.
>
> —Czeslaw Milosz

> When hit by boredom go for it. Let yourself be crushed by it, *submerge, hit bottom.* In general with things unpleasant the rule is, the sooner you hit bottom, the faster you surface.
>
> —Joseph Brodsky

To fall and hit bottom life has to give up its hold on the horizontal, its restriction to the same level in a now tedious hierarchy. For this, there's no choice but to descend, if only because hatred, that forgotten structure inside boredom, has already failed in its attempt to rise above history and circumstance. Upward progress is a social or economic idea, but from literature and, to an extent, religion, we know going down holds a lot of life's interesting possibilities. If up isn't an option, then down is the obvious alternative; it's even desirable. Down is the direction poetry travels on the page, anyway, and poets have tended to follow their pens. For contrast, the etymology of the word *prose* means to go forward, generally straight forward, and there's nothing internal to a sentence that limits its length or sideways nature. Paragraphing arranges ideas logically, but for that one could imagine a codex like an accordion, the folds expanding laterally. Even punctuation isn't really about organizing or shaping the inherently horizontal character of prose. Periods, commas, and colons regulate the breath, and well-written prose always includes, in its long or short rhythms, a kind of pulmonary function; reaching into these vital rhythms, good prose can, like breathing exercises in yoga, inhabit the visceral life of a reader. Conceivably prose could be written on ribbons hundreds of yards long, winding the reader and testing his lungs in another way, but we bind and store it in books, mainly, so that doesn't happen. The quotidian tendency of prose is either to satisfy an immediate disposable need or to point beyond itself, toward a distant, receding horizon of information. It's the *écriture* of choice for assembling bicycles and analyzing wars, and the difficulty for a writer, the danger, is that his words, failing to capture a cadent, living pulse, will lose meaning in the vastness of other words. If a piece of prose aspires to art, it must close itself off, setting in motion sympathetic vibrations and gaining, as with any enclosure, resonance.

Poetry's orientation is not primarily horizontal but vertical. It goes across, left to right, but mostly it goes down, top to bottom, and that descent is dictated from within. Though our language for prosody has largely shifted to a discussion of stresses, we still listen for feet and measure in meter the distance a line travels. The syllables in a haiku might be the exception to this idea of poetry's descent, but you'd lose the stillness in space if all seventeen were strung like clothesline across the page. While a haiku hangs, suspended in air, hexameter hits its beats and heads down, line by line, and it's easy to imagine an idea of descent and depth coming to a stymied poet by simply staring disconsolately at the page. The etymology of *verse* means to turn or return, and if the trick in prose is to overcome its diffuse and vague and ubiquitous presence, the trap for poetry is hermeticism, its tendency toward the occult, the ease with which it turns in on itself and, going down, abandons or forfeits its participation in the upper world. Still, poetry has no choice about its generally chthonic direction. Even a democratic poet like Whitman, resisting hierarchy's vertical axis with his broad, barbaric yawp, eventually descends. Down is where poetry is, and whatever poetry has to say, whatever it can deliver, is down there too.

In a trope typical of him, at least in this poem, Hugo monkeys with the expected syntactical arrangement, wrenching new emphasis from fairly accessible language; playing with inflection is a way he has of torquing a phrase, and he does it twice in the second stanza. Let me look at the second instance first. The mill "in collapse/for fifty years that won't *fall finally down*" gives us the adverb in its most active form. *Finally* doesn't idle in an ancillary place, taking up slack because the right verb wasn't available. In fact, for a word without a verbal form (except the somewhat bureaucratic "finalize"), *finally*, as Hugo writes it, is as close as you're going to get to a sense of the desire inside the downward trajectory of falling. Somehow the "down" here, the collapse, is being propped up, penultimately supported by an old, useless structure, and "finally" is the hope or possibility of falling, the fulfillment of fifty years of need. Positioned just above a stanza composed entirely of questions, the line suggests that the mill, slumped in desuetude, must give way before a bottom can be revealed. The end of Pburg (as locals call the town) or history or gray isn't really the end—there's something below. But to get to it the landscape's first got to be leveled, the kilns and the mill razed, the horizontal world abandoned.

"All memory resolves itself in gaze"—this is the second instance of oddly inflected syntax, and it's an interesting choice. Omitting the expected article creates a slight hitch in the reading, compelling attention, and compresses the word *gaze*, making it do the work of both noun and verb, mixing stasis and action, fusing space and time—the word is like a pivot, and the entire stanza turns on the phrase, bringing us to a fatal form of memory, an arrested, fixed memory that is now the only thing preventing total collapse, while at the same time offering *gaze*—gazing—as an action that might release the hold memory has on the horizontal. It's at this point in the poem that Hugo begins the move toward the salvational hopes of language, of poetry itself. He's down low, but not low enough yet to find his poem.

It seems to me a poet of Hugo's skill and knowledge can't possibly write this line without hearing the allusion to Orpheus. This is the heart of the poem, this is where it is. It happens quickly, reading like a toss-off, without a glance back, but I believe it's there. *Gaze* shows up in a similar passage in *The Merchant of Venice*, also about Orpheus, also about the poet's power to alter the quality of perception: "Their savage eyes turn'd to a modest gaze/By the sweet power of music: therefore the poet/Did feign that Orpheus . . ." Orpheus, whose lyre is now among the stars, is the figure of the poet and the poet's work. Nothing can withstand the charms of his music. Beasts are softened and lose their ferocity, stolid oaks move closer just to hear, rocks relax their hardness. Here it's probably worth mentioning—actually, vital to understanding—that Hugo's poem sits on top of the pastoral tradition, and certainly could be looked at as a failed bucolic. The poem seems to turn by shorthanding this rich, deep tradition. In Virgil's *Georgics* the story of Orpheus shows up strangely, in a treatise on bees, but has the passing character of a fertility myth. That the "green" in Hugo's poem is only "panoramic" at this point indicates how far from the regenerative power of all these vegetable myths Philipsburg is: there's no real sustenance in a panorama—or, as they say in Montana, you can't eat the scenery.

More important to Hugo's poem than the wide horizontal panorama is the idea of descent and depth implied in the Orpheus myth. Both are orders of vision, but they offer different things. Ovid gives Virgil's Orpheus a fuller treatment, the one people are familiar with, in which Eurydice, after her wedding to the poet, flees a seducer (Aristaeus, another poet and, not surprisingly, a beekeeper, who will subsequently suffer an apiary disaster) and is bitten by a snake and dies. Orpheus descends into the underworld to reclaim his bride. Along the way a fairy feeds him roasted ants, a flea's thigh, butterflies' brains, mites, a rainbow tart, all to be washed down with dewdrops and beer made of barleycorn—indicating, fabulously, the earthy depth of the poet's descent. In the underworld, as in the upper air, Orpheus sings his grief, and ghosts shed tears, Sisyphus sits on his rock to listen, Ixion's wheel stops its ceaseless revolving, Tantalus forgets his thirst, and the Furies, just this once, cry. But on his way back to the world, in an exact, cautionary lesson about one of the perils of artistic creation, Orpheus turns around, hoping to assure himself, and loses his wife, who reaches out for a last embrace as she's drawn back toward death. Orpheus gives it another shot, but the underworld, whether in Chicago or Hades, is famously unforgiving, and second chances aren't available. In mourning, Orpheus seems to sicken with ennui, yet plays his lyre, wooing the inanimate world, wresting emotion from the trees and rocks, but eventually, forgoing women and loving boys, he's torn apart during a Bacchanalia by jealous Thracian maidens, and his severed head floats down the Hebrus, while his lyre, his poetry, is flung to the heavens.

If what distinguishes us from other members of the animal kingdom is speech, then literature—and poetry in particular, being the highest form of locution—is, to put it bluntly, the goal of our species.

—Joseph Brodsky

What's the deal with a poet who fills an entire stanza, fully a fourth of his poem, with questions? Part of it's just Hugo's standard battering style—where a single question might do, he pounds out a whole stanza—but again, that style serves the subject. The heavy questions hammer away and demolish the mill that won't collapse. That Hugo's prosodic fist is big and blunt only makes it more suitable for the job. Each question—about the persistence of love, the pain of defeat, the scorn preventing desire—undercuts not only the binding failures of Philipsburg but also the poem's earlier assertions, turning us toward a kind of metacreation. The best way to come at this understanding is through the poem's back door. Desire in this stanza has an anachronistic, distinctly World War II flavor, with its blondes, booze, and jazz, and you sense Hugo's own swaggering, wounded self, his own haunting self-doubt, his own town, Seattle, needing to die inside. Suddenly it's no longer 1907 but 1947, and Hugo is back from the war, reaching down into a pain and hope that's personal. That's fine; it's his poem, after all. This slight historical warp is partly about Hugo's generous self-effacement, anyway; but it's also an oblique admission about the stake he has in the poem. In seeking hope for Philipsburg he begins to find hope for himself or, more accurately, for his poem. Here's the motivation, the stirring of desire, the first turn toward feeling necessary again. In much the same way the myth of Orpheus elaborates a secondary tale about the act of creation, Hugo too gives us a poem about the making of poetry. The poem offers, somewhat covertly, an allegory of the poet's soul, caught in the terrifying process of creation. Why would anyone write a poem in this wrecked world? And really, how could they? Massive doubt, failed love, shitty thoughts, empty spirit, a dead history compelling a transfixed vision, these are devastations that might overwhelm and silence anyone; and silence, for a poet, is a prison. It's where the descent hits bottom, it's where the poet either faces or does not face all the risks of failed comprehension. It makes sense that Hugo would discover his reason for writing in a stanza so completely expressive of doubt. The critical difference between a poet and a regular citizen is that the poet seeks this realm; it's where he works, where his office is.

So, why questions? Everything in this stanza could be written using the indicative, flatly observed, or the ragging, hortatory imperative of a coach, urging us on. One answer might be that questions imply an auditor, the presence of another, and a stanza full of them suggests, by reaching out, some break in the isolation. Perhaps the questions are meant to prod an answer, but I kind of don't think so. Answers are as transient and foolish as we are, and poets generally aren't in the solution business. In fact, if you're a poet and you're going to pose questions, they'd better approach the unanswerable. Why? Is it that only questions without answers are worth asking? Is it that the muse needs courting and doesn't usually go with know-it-alls and wise guys? Is it that questions salt and preserve life, keeping the mystery fresh? Is it that any descent that hopes to claim our attention and hence a place in the record books is asterisked by answers, as if the poet, cheating, hadn't really touched bottom? In poetry, is the irritable reaching after answers (or certainties, as Keats put it) paradoxically just a type of doubt, a doubt about poetry itself? If rock bottom, if total bust for a poet is silence, then the questions must be unanswerable, without remedy, to provoke the central event, which is language. Answers are the end of speech, not the beginning, and if language is the main draw in poetry, silence is the occasion for it, the ground of renewal. Questions precede speech, they're language tensely coiled, expectant.

In the second stanza, the word *hatred* repeats, and now in the third stanza, it's *ring* we hear twice. It's an excellent, nearly echoic repetition, it rings, but it's also a curious choice; every connotation I can think of is almost purely positive. Clarity and resonance, calling, summons, proclamations, talk, producing sound, vibration, sonority— all meanings that counter the unanswerable questions, the testing of silence in the stanza. In my reading the aural quality of the word creates tension, making music of a different tenor than the literal subject. My ear hears something my eye doesn't quite see. The sound of *ring* rides on the surface of the stanza, separating from it somewhat. Whereas *hatred* draws us down into the core of the poem, *ring* begins to lift us out of it. Down deep in this stanza of questions, we hear a ringing, and it becomes possible to understand that Hugo's questions, their Orphic summons, aren't calling for an answer; they're calling for poetry.

How can one write poetry after Auschwitz?

—critic Theodor Adorno

And how can one eat lunch?

—poet Mark Strand

"Say no to yourself"—if only Orpheus had, if only he'd refused the unsure, doubting, rearward glance, he'd have spent that first night back in the upper air abed with his bride. Instead, his hesitation breaks the lyric charm and condemns Eurydice to death. The temptation, in art as well as life, is to fall back on old forms, to attempt an impossible repetition, giving yourself over to the sort of redundancy that has always been the defining feature of the underworld, where time is either a torment or means nothing because the iterations are endless and unvarying.

Hell is crowded not because sinners are common-
place but because incompletion is the norm. Orpheus,
descending, charms the underworld, he moves it toward
an uncharacteristic stillness and rest, but in ascending, it's
as if his hesitation, his glance back, were suddenly an afflic-
tion no different from the thirst of Tantalus or the labor of
Sisyphus. Looking back, losing his bride, his work remains
unfinished, forever, and the sorrow he can't overcome
results in a sort of hypnotic hindsight. Saying no is necessary; it too is part of the process of creation. After saying
yes to the descent, saying no is how the poet emerges.
Perhaps another way of articulating this is to say that a new
yes must be found, the courage of the descent sustained until
it's completed. In a poem the future, or the next couple
dozen words anyway (which to a poet is the same thing),
is the poem. The need is finally aesthetic. Hugo's final stanza
is a return to speech, referenced phrasally throughout: *say
no, he says, you tell, you're talking*. But the return is premised
on not looking back, on avoiding the gaze that tempts and
paralyzes memory. Unlike Orpheus, the poet here says no
and, in true Western fashion, gets the girl, who happens to
be slender, with red hair that lights the wall.

It's not the sort of refusal it might first seem—seemed
to me, anyway. It's not a turning away, an opting out of
history, an easy escape. To push the metapoetic reading,
the car, that absent term from the first stanza, still runs, as
does life, but on this newly accessed level of understanding,

I think it's also fair to say that another of the missing, implied terms is poetry itself. Poetry is the vehicle that broke down and brought Hugo here, to the degrees of gray, but it still runs, and the proof is the poem itself. The poem is what the poet brings back, that's his fortune. You can imagine these words lost among broken symbols, dragged off by history, sunk in silence, but that isn't what we have. Not answers but aesthetic pressure completes the poem. In the end, it doesn't matter that the light reveals a wall that will likely never come down entirely. "Let us not look for the door, and the way out," Camus wrote, "anywhere but in the wall against which we are living." The irony, the slight undertone pulling at Hugo's last word, tempers the jubilance with a doubt, but suggests that in this prison, shared by all, life is still possible. Fortuna is sometimes depicted wearing a blindfold, and the light in the final line really refers to the act of seeing. It's about optics more than opportunity. The poem is the light.

Tonight was the Fourth of July, and another order of light was at work, flaring in the sky over these same streets. It was a disorganized display, mostly people in their back-yards firing rockets that shot up, burst, fell, and faded, somewhat emptily, in this vast valley. I walked to town because I needed to double-check the streets of Philipsburg and square what I saw with the falling man's incomprehensible descent. I wanted to think just a little more about Hugo and the place of poetry in the face of terrible things. I stopped by a green house above Main Street where, all last winter, dogs fought over the carcasses of several deer. I remembered the rib cages marbled red and white with blood and fat and the ruts of stained red snow where the warring dogs dragged the bones, but when I passed by tonight I saw the house had been boarded up, the tenant gone in a going that doesn't really hold much mystery, not here in Philipsburg. What's another absence, another vacancy? But if this uncelebrated loss means nothing, I can't see how the falling man's descent acquires true significance either. Consensus isn't an answer. Mining towns in Montana or Kentucky that have collapsed over the course of a century have suffered a descent as murderous as a moment in New York, but history has hidden those deaths and numbed the witnesses and litanized their loss under the rubric of progress. In the case of Philipsburg, only a poet spoke out, from his own isolation, to say something about the devastating pain.

Still, ruin, nearly as much as a good poem, is strangely enduring. The hills behind Philipsburg are full of things that have failed to remain upright. Poets might not save, but the clichés surrounding September 11 didn't stop anything either, and in this sense the score, in the game of language, is decisively on the side of poetry. If forced to choose between failures, poetry is probably the better one. The difference between the truth and a cliché is the difference between what we really know and what we've all heard about. That diversity is good is a slogan we've all heard, but it has expressive limits—it's not okay to fly jets into office buildings—and so what does it really mean? For me, borrowing from Isaiah Berlin, another writer intimately aware of history, diversity (or plurality) is an answer to the central twentieth-century historical problem of radical subjectivity. Accumulating enough subjectivities—setting them against each other—is as close as we're going to come to objectivity, and this is why agreement is problematic: what's the point of being right if it's only safety in numbers? The history of being right and how wrong it's turned out to be is a long one. By this measure the terrorists were wrong—such empty holiness is almost too much to bear in mind—but when being right provides comfort, when the sensation of it is pleasant, when it allays anxiety or lends security, then it seems to be doing the job of ignorance. If we're right, then the nature and quality and burden of being right is our issue. Now it seems time to argue for the tragic or the absurd, for anything that tempers and draws limits. Sometimes contradiction can't be resolved away and then it becomes the new reality and there's no way out. The falling man is enormously sad and insignificant, he is everything as well as nothing. The only way into his descent is through our solitude. Patriotism's just a rag we fly over the silence.

In *Mimesis*, Erich Auerbach's book on the representation of reality in Western literature, he talks of the shift from antiquity to a New Testament style of realism. "To be sure," he writes, "we must not forget that the transformation is here one whose course progresses to somewhere outside of history, to the end of time or to the coincidence of all times, in other words upward, and does not . . . remain on the horizontal plane of historical events." I wonder, was our understanding of September 11 little more than a Christian homily, an escape from history, a romance secularizing the divine or lifting the legend out of the ruin—is that where it all went? All through the writing of this I thought of Shelley, who at eighteen sent copies of a pamphlet on atheism to every professor at Oxford. He believed a university dedicated to open discussion and the free exchange of ideas would be interested. He was kicked out. Next he went to Ireland, planning to begin a major rehabilitation of all mankind by organizing the Irish into a "society of peace and love," perhaps a doomed enterprise. Next he was off to Wales, again with a pamphlet, this one called "A Declaration of Rights." He enclosed copies in dark green bottles which he sealed with wax and cast into the ocean; other copies he floated aloft, to be blown inland on balloons. Is it reasonable to think Shelley was eternally part of mankind in his solitary foolish hope at sea's edge? That his solitude was the mark of a deeper, broader inclusion? Or is this just poetic fancy? Watching the fireworks made me wonder. In general I don't care for activities—fireworks or football or movies—where large groups of people gather and look at the same thing. This is probably just a queerness of temperament. Maybe I don't like crowds. Regardless, the fireworks rose up, pulsing in our local cosmos. On the way home I stopped to watch the show with some kids who were heaped under blankets while the parents handled the pyrotechnics. Each explosion eclipsed the sky with dazzling colors and froze the onlooking, upturned faces like a strobe. All the kids kept pointing up, the way astonished kids will, as if I might not know where to look.

From The Spirit of History

When gold paint flakes from the arms of sculptures,
When the letter falls out of the book of laws,
Then consciousness is naked as an eye.

When the pages of books fall in fiery scraps
Onto smashed leaves and twisted metal,
The tree of good and evil is stripped bare.

When a wing made of canvas is extinguished
In a potato patch, when steel disintegrates,
Nothing is left but straw and cow dung.

———

I rolled a cigarette and licked the paper.
Then a match in the little house of my hand.
And why not a tinderbox with a flint?
The wind was blowing. I sat on the road at noon,
Thinking and thinking. Beside me, potatoes.

— Czeslaw Milosz

Also available from Clear Cut Press:

The Clear Cut Future
edited by Clear Cut Press
CCP 000 / 528 pp.   ISBN 0-9723234-1-4
With color and B&W illustrations
$12.95

This anthology maps the territory of interest to Clear Cut Press, more or less. Among the contributors are writers Stacey Levine, Charles D'Ambrosio, Emily White, Rebecca Brown, Robert Glück, Pravin Jain (a former Enron executive), Casey Sanchez (a fish slimer), painter Michael Brophy, and photographers Robert Adams and Ari Marcopoulos.

Ode to certain interstates and Other Poems
by Howard W. Robertson
CCP 001 / 184 pp.   ISBN 0-9723234-2-2
$12.95

From 1995-96, Eugene, Oregon, poet Howard W. Robertson worked as a long-haul truck driver in the eleven Western states and British Columbia, an experience that inspired the thirteen-part title poem in this collection. In 2003, he was awarded the Robinson Jeffers Tor House Prize for Poetry.

*Occasional Work and Seven Walks from the
Office for Soft Architecture*
by Lisa Robertson
CCP 002 / 274 pp. ISBN 0-9723234-3-0
With color illustrations
$12.95

Since 1996, poet Lisa Robertson (*XEclogue, Debbie: An
Epic, The Weather*) has used the Office for Soft Architecture
as an apparatus for lyrical research focused primarily on
Vancouver, B.C. This collection of essays considers such subjects as public fountains, pleasure-grounds, bridges, gardens,
office towers, suburbs, shrubs, restaurants, and motion.

Denny Smith
stories by Robert Glück
CCP 003 / 268 pp. ISBN 0-9723234-4-9
$12.95

These new stories by the author of *Margery Kempe, Jack the
Modernist,* and *Reader* use events in the life of their author,
such as burglary, sex, reading, conversation, humiliation,
child raising, and porn, as a ground for the expansion of
empathy and intellect. Self-absorbed, the stories are also
profoundly communal. Michel Foucault esteemed Glück
as one of the world's finest writers about sex.

Core Sample: Portland Art Now
edited by Randy Gragg and Matthew Stadler
CCP 004 / 416 pp. ISBN 0-9723234-8-1
With color illustrations and DVD
$15.95

Core Sample was an artist-initiated, citywide exhibition
of contemporary art that took place in Portland, Oregon,
in October 2003. This catalog documents Core Sample's
methods and results and serves as a practical guide to the
mobilization of noninstitutional cultures and a reflection on
the worth of such projects. With essays by Lynne Tillman,
Lawrence Rinder, Cecilia Dougherty, and Peter Culley.

Shoot the Buffalo
by Matt Briggs
CCP 006 / 520 pp. ISBN 0-9723234-7-3
$14.95

This first novel from the author of *The Remains of River
Names* is the recollection of a boy raised by hippies, a trac-
ing of his life's story from improvised childhood in and
around Seattle through young adulthood, when he joins
the military.

Frances Johnson
by Stacey Levine
CCP 007 / 270 pp.   ISBN 0-9723234-6-5
$12.95

A new novel from the PEN Western Fiction Prize-winning author of *Dra__* and *My Horse and other stories*, this is the story of a woman living in a small town in Florida who can't decide whether or not to attend the town dance.